The Heart of it All

The Heart of it All

The Bible's Big Picture

Samuel Wells

CANTERBURY
PRESS

Norwich

© Samuel Wells 2019

First published in 2019 by the Canterbury Press Norwich

Editorial office : 3rd Floor, Invicta House,108–114 Golden Lane,

London EC1Y 0TG, UK

www.canterburypress.co.uk

Canterbury Press is an imprint of Hymns Ancient & Modern Ltd

(a registered charity)

Hymns Ancient & Modern* is a registered trademark of Hymns Ancient &
Modern Ltd 13A Hellesdon Park Road, Norwich, Norfolk NR6 5DR, UK

British Library Cataloguing in Publication data
A catalogue record for this book is available
from the British Library

978 1-78622-225-1

Printed and bound in Great Britain by
CPI Group (UK) Ltd

For

Walter Brueggemann

Ellen Davis

Richard Hays

and

Ched Myers

Contents

Preface

How can anyone have the temerity to abridge the holy scriptures and presume to render the heart of their truth in a narrative one-thirtieth of their length? This is not intended as an immodest volume, but I understand the reticence that might inhibit many from setting about such a project. Yet Christians in different ways abridge the scriptures every time they preach the gospel, write theology, teach the faith, say the creed, or seek to win the heart of their neighbour. And a great many Christians feel embarrassed that they could not confidently summarize the story, or attempt to put key elements, especially of the Old Testament, in narrative sequence, still less relate their significance to other parts of the Bible or derive wisdom from research about when these words were written and why. Those who know their Bible from back to front may not need a guide such as this. But I have written it for those who would gain a greater understanding of the shape and nuance and interrelatedness of the story – and for any who, familiar with the order of the books as conventionally set out, would be glad to reflect further on the theological significance of how the story unfolds.

I have called it *The Heart of it All* because, without pretending it includes every vital or memorable part of scripture, I'm seeking to make a virtue of its brevity and, in the restrictions of length, striving to identify the very soul of the story. I believe

Christianity is primarily a relationship, or a set of relationships, between God, church, kingdom, creation and self; and like any relationship, it can't be contained by or reduced to words. Likewise the Bible is a collection of 66 books, some of which – like Isaiah or Psalms – appear themselves to be collections of sayings, songs or stories. This volume isn't an attempt to contain or reduce those 66 books, but to speak of their diversity and unity, and in the process go to the heart of it all.

I don't seek to imitate the shape in which the Bible is conventionally ordered, from Genesis to the maps. Instead I surmise that the Old Testament was born in the crucible of exile, and so I begin with what I regard as the definitive story of exile, that of the three men in the fiery furnace from the book of Daniel. The question the Old Testament is fundamentally asking is: if God has made us a covenant partner forever, what are we doing in Babylon? Likewise I begin the second part of the narrative with Paul in Rome, in a similar quandary: if God has released us from the power of sin and death through the death and resurrection of Christ, why am I in chains? The central insight of this book is that both testaments came to be written for broadly similar reasons: the question of present adversity in the midst of eternal blessing. In the Commentary that follows Parts One and Two I explore in greater depth such questions and the judgements I have made in shaping the story. In the Epilogue, I seek to show how the story may be brought together in a succinct and compelling way. And in the short Study Guide, I offer suggestions for how readers can ponder the depth of the story, alone or together.

It goes without saying that there's a lot missing. I don't apologize for that. I hope what is here does justice to the breadth and depth of the whole, while highlighting the signature elements and, through narrative structure, connecting those elements in helpful and illuminating ways. I make no claim to offer a definitive shape: if my humble attempt stimulates others to render their own equivalent version, that will be a sign of success, not failure. I'm grateful for a conversation with Simon Russell Beale that initiated the project, for dialogues with Jo Wells, Rebekah Eklund, Maureen Knudsen Langdoc, Ray Barfield and Stanley Hauerwas that have enhanced it, and for the engagement of the Theology Group at St Martin-in-the-Fields, who read the manuscript together. The book is dedicated to four disciples, friends, scholars and prophets who have taught me that it's not about my learning to read the Bible, it's about letting the Bible read me.

My greatest hope is that, like Thomas looking into and touching the wounds of the risen Jesus, the reader will come to the end of this short work, and be overcome by the wonder and grace of its true author, and exclaim, 'My Lord and my God.'

Part One

1

Fire, Water and Wilderness

First there was the fire. We were in Babylon. King Nebuchadnezzar ruled the world from Babylon. He had satraps, prefects, governors and counsellors. He had treasurers, justices, magistrates and officials in every province.

But Nebuchadnezzar wanted to be sure of his people's loyalty. He made a golden statue. Not a calf, like our ancestors made at the foot of Sinai; but a 90-foot statue of himself. 'O peoples, nations, and languages,' the herald comprehensively proclaimed, 'listen for the sound of the horn, pipe, lyre, trigon, harp, and drum.' What a cacophony that was. 'Then,' shouted the herald, 'fall down and worship the golden statue!' There never was such a gathering of people since the tower of Babel. But there was a threat. 'Whoever refuses shall immediately be thrown into a blazing furnace.'

Shadrach, Meshach and Abednego were Jews. But they held government office. They heard the sound of the horn, pipe, lyre, trigon, harp and drum. But they did not bow down. Nebuchadnezzar was furious. He said, 'If you do not worship, you shall be thrown into a blazing furnace. And what god will deliver you from my hands then?' Shadrach, Meshach and Abednego replied, 'If our God delivers us, well and good. But even if our God does not, we will still not serve your gods and we will still not worship your golden statue'; whereupon Shadrach, Meshach and Abednego were hurled into the furnace of blazing fire. King Nebuchadnezzar looked on in amazement. He exclaimed, 'I thought we threw three men, bound, into the fire? But in the flames I see four men walking. They're not bound. They're not harmed. And the fourth looks like a god.'

The prophet Isaiah wrote, 'You'll pass through waters, and I'll be with you. You'll cross rivers, yet they'll not overwhelm you. You'll walk through fire, but you won't be burned – and the flames shan't consume you.' It turned out Babylon wasn't a water that overwhelmed us, or a fire that consumed us; it was a fire that refined us and a water that baptized us.

Then there was the water. In Babylon we remembered the water of chaos – the beginning of all things. God created heaven and earth. The earth was formless. Darkness covered the face of the deep. A wind from God hovered over the waters. God said, 'Light': there was light. God said, 'Dome': and there was a dome in the midst of the waters, separating the waters. God said, 'Land': and dry land appeared as the waters under the sky gathered in one place. God said, 'Likeness': and God made humankind, with dominion over the creatures of the sea and the air. So humankind was created in God's image: male and female. God blessed them. God said to them, 'Be fruitful. Multiply. Fill the earth.' When it was the seventh day God blessed it and hallowed it, and rested from all the work of creation. So on the seventh day we too bless, and hallow, and rest.

But from Babylon we looked back also on the water of liberation. That water also began with fire. God met Moses at Mount Horeb in a flame of fire out of a bush. Moses looked: the bush blazed – yet it was not consumed. God called to Moses from the bush, 'Moses, Moses!' Moses said, 'Here I am.' Then God said, 'Come no closer! Remove the sandals from your feet. You stand on holy ground.' Moses hid his face, for he was afraid to behold God. Then God said, 'I have seen the misery of my people in Egypt. Their cry has reached me. I have seen how the Egyptians oppress them. I know their sufferings. I have come down to deliver them, and bring them up out of that land to a good and broad land, a land flowing with milk and honey, to the country of the Canaanites, the Hittites, the Amorites, the Perizzites, the Hivites, and the Jebusites.' But Moses said to God, 'Who am I to do all this?' God said, 'I shall be with you; and when you have brought the people out of Egypt, I shall bring you back here to this mountain.' Moses asked, 'What is your name?' God answered, 'I am who I am. This is my name for ever.'

When the moment came for us to be led out, Moses called the elders of Israel and said to them, 'Everyone, select a lamb. Eat it tonight with unleavened bread and bitter herbs. Eat it quickly, ready to depart: tuck the hem of your tunic into your girdle, put sandals on your feet, and take a staff in your hand. Take a hyssop, dip it in the lamb's blood that's in the basin, and touch the lintel and the two doorposts with the blood. Don't go outside until morning. The Lord will pass over you and strike down the firstborn of the Egyptians; but seeing the blood the Lord will pass over your door.'

Then we hastened to the Red Sea. The Lord went in front of us in a pillar of cloud by day, to lead us, and in a pillar of fire by night, to lighten our path. Neither the pillar of cloud nor the pillar of fire left its place in front of us.

The Lord hardened the heart of Pharaoh, king of Egypt.

Pharaoh pursued us, his horses, chariots, chariot drivers and army. We looked back and could see the Egyptians closing on us. We were terrified. We cried out to Moses, 'Was it because there were no graves in Egypt that you brought us to die in the wilderness? We would have preferred to serve the Egyptians than die like this.' But Moses said to us, 'Don't be afraid. Stand firm. The Lord will save you today. The Egyptians you see today you shall never see again. The Lord will fight for you. You have only to keep still.'

Then the Lord said to Moses, 'Raise up your staff, and stretch out your hand over the sea and divide it, that the Israelites may cross the sea on dry ground.' We went into the sea on dry ground, the waters forming a wall for us to right and left. The Egyptians pursued; all of Pharaoh's horses, chariots and chariot drivers came into the sea after us. The waters returned and covered Pharaoh's entire army; not one of them remained. The Egyptians lay dead on the seashore.

So water of chaos became order and water of slavery became freedom. After Moses died, God said to Joshua, 'Be strong and courageous: for I am with you wherever you go.' As Joshua crossed the Jordan, we discovered that water was our way to order and freedom. When Joshua came to the river, the priests bearing the ark of the covenant were in front of us. But when they dipped their feet in the edge of the water, the waters flowing from above stood still, rising up in a single heap. Then we could cross the river opposite Jericho. While we were crossing, the priests who carried the ark of the covenant stood on dry ground in the middle of the river, until our entire nation finished crossing the Jordan.

But there was not just the refiner's fire; there were not just the waters that filled the earth. There was something else: the dust of the wilderness. The wilderness was the place we went when we'd left slavery but hadn't yet entered the Promised Land. It was where we learned the disciplines of freedom. It was where we discovered what it meant to depend on God. We complained to Moses. We said, 'If only we'd died in Egypt, where we had food. Here in the wilderness we're so hungry!' Moses said he would rain bread from heaven for us, and on the sixth day we should gather twice as much. The glory of the Lord appeared in the cloud and confirmed Moses' words. Then those of us who gathered much had nothing over, and those of us who gathered little had no shortage. We tried to keep a surplus for the next day but it went rotten – except on the seventh day, when the worms stayed away. Even then some of us went out looking for manna, though we found none; Moses was so angry with us. We went on eating that manna for 40 years.

The wilderness was where we found out who we were and who God was. In the wilderness we recalled a single night that embodied our whole story. Our forefather Jacob was alone; and a man wrestled with him until daybreak. The man didn't defeat Jacob, but he still put Jacob's hip out of its socket. Jacob said to the man, 'I won't let you go, unless you bless me.' Jacob realized he'd seen God face to face, and yet his life had been preserved. He'd striven with God and with humans, and prevailed. At that moment Jacob became Israel, each one of us. Israel: it means struggling with God, and being blessed. That's how we discovered that we were as important to God as God was to us. And we realized that all our struggles were, in the end, struggles with God.

2

Covenant

It turned out that fire, water and wilderness were all about preparation. They were like a quest that taught us about ourselves and the thing we were heading towards. At Sinai we discovered what that thing was. There God told us why we were made, why we were saved, why we were borne up on eagles' wings and what our purpose was. These were God's words: 'You shall be my treasured possession out of all the peoples. The whole earth is mine, but you shall be for me a priestly kingdom and a holy nation.' These precious words were shrouded in thunder and lightning. There was thick cloud on the mountain, and a trumpet-blast so loud that we all trembled. Meanwhile the whole mountain shook violently. God was about to make a covenant with us. This was the moment we found out our destiny.

God told us how to keep that covenant. 'Have no other gods: one is all you need. Make no idols: I am enough for you. Revere my name: nothing is more important than me. Keep the Sabbath: your security lies in me. Honour your parents: you did not put yourself here. Respect life: you belong to me. Respect marriage: your loyalty to one another reflects your fidelity to me. Respect property: I will ensure you have what you need. Respect truth: it will set you free. Curtail your craving: let all your desires become a longing for me.' Here we discovered the meaning of justice: justice is our covenant commitment to reflect back to God a life that corresponds with God's faithfulness to us. The two stone tablets of those commandments became the ark of the covenant; and the ark of the covenant became our way of knowing God was with us.

At this most holy moment, the covenant of the law, we remembered an earlier covenant, the covenant of life, that God made with our forefather Noah, when only eight people and an ark full of animals survived the deluge, but after which God said, 'Never again will I curse the ground because of humankind, nor will I ever again destroy every living creature as I have done. As long as the earth endures, seedtime and harvest, cold and heat, summer and winter, day and night, shall never cease.' And we remembered another covenant, the covenant of the land, that God made with our forefather Abraham. To Abraham God said, 'Go to the land that I will show you. I will make of you a great nation, and I will bless you, and make your name great, so that you will be a blessing. In you all the families of the earth shall find blessing.' We are possessed by God, that through us all nations will know God's blessing.

Under Moses we discovered that our security came only from God. Meanwhile to Abraham it was revealed that God would provide. God said to Abraham, 'Take your son, your only son Isaac, whom you love, and offer him as a burnt offering.' So Abraham rose early, and took his son. On the third day he looked up and saw the place. Isaac said, 'Father!' And Abraham said, 'Here I am, my son.' Isaac said, 'The fire and the wood are here, but where is the lamb for a burnt offering?' Abraham said, 'God will provide, my son.' Abraham bound Isaac and reached out his hand to kill his son. But the angel of the Lord called, 'Abraham!

Do not lay your hand on the boy or do anything to him; for now I know that you fear God, since you have not withheld your son, your only son, from me.' And Abraham looked up and saw a ram, caught in a thicket. Abraham took the ram and offered it as a burnt offering instead of his son. The Lord provides for those who trust the covenant. The covenant is who God is and who we are.

Time and again when all was stripped away and all we had was God, however perilous our plight, God was more than enough for everything we needed. As Joshua took hold of the Promised Land, he came to Jericho. The Lord said, 'You shall march around the city for six days, all the warriors circling, with seven priests bearing seven trumpets of rams' horns before the ark. On the seventh day you shall march around the city seven times, the priests blowing the trumpets. When they make a long blast with the ram's horn, then all the people shall shout with a great shout; and the wall of the city will fall down flat.' And so it was. We all shouted, the wall fell down flat, and we charged into the city and captured it.

Again, when we were in jeopardy in the Promised Land, the angel of the Lord called Gideon to be our judge. God told Gideon to send most of his troops away, lest we think we'd defeated Midian by our own hand. So the fearful among us left, 22,000 of them, leaving 10,000 by Gideon's side. But there were still too many, so God chose just the ones who lapped water like a dog rather than knelt down to drink, and only 300 remained. Gideon led the 300 to the Midianites' camp, holding trumpets and empty jars, with torches inside the jars. We blew the trumpets and smashed the jars that were in our hands. The Lord set everyone's sword against their fellow and against all the army. And the Midianites cried out and fled.

Yet still we forgot the covenant and turned away from God. Until there came Samson. Samson killed a lion with his bare hands. He slaughtered 30 men of Ashkelon. He broke out of the chains of imprisonment and killed a thousand Philistines with the fresh jawbone of a donkey. Yet he loved Delilah. Delilah pleaded to discover the secret of his strength. Samson said, 'If my head were shaved, I would become weak, like anyone else.' So she had his seven locks of hair cut while he slept. The Philistines seized him and gouged out his eyes. They brought him down to Gaza and bound him with bronze shackles; and he ground at the mill in the prison. But his hair began to grow back. When the Philistines gathered to offer sacrifice, they brought in Samson to ridicule him. On the roof there were 3,000 men and women, who looked on while Samson performed. Then Samson grasped the two middle pillars on which the building rested, and the building fell on the Philistines. So he killed more at his death than he killed during his life.

3

King and Temple

Until the time of Samson the covenant meant one thing above all: the land – and freedom and plenty within it. But from this moment on we began to realize the covenant meant other things; four in particular. The first was a person. Hannah longed for a child. She made this vow: 'O Lord of hosts, if only you will look on the misery of your servant, and will give me a male child, then I will give him to you, and he will remain yours for ever.' Eli the priest thought at first she was drunk. But God granted her petition. And she bore a son. She named him Samuel.

Samuel grew and came to lead us. Our elders came to Samuel and said, 'Give us a king to govern us, like other nations.' The Lord told Samuel, 'They have not rejected you, but they have rejected me from being king over them.' Samuel said to us, 'The king will take the best of your fields, vineyards and olive orchards. He will take a tenth of your grain. He will take a tenth of your flocks. You shall be his slaves.' But we refused to listen. The Lord said, 'Listen to their voice and give them a king.'

Then the Lord said to Samuel, 'I will send to you a man from the land of Benjamin, and you shall anoint him to rule my people Israel. He shall save my people from the Philistines; for I have seen the suffering of my people; their outcry has come to me.' When

Samuel found Saul, Saul said, 'I am only a Benjaminite, from the least of the tribes of Israel, and my family is the humblest of all the families of the tribe of Benjamin.' Nonetheless Samuel poured a phial of oil on his head, and kissed him. We all went to Gilgal, and there we made Saul king before the Lord. Thus did we find a king to represent God's covenant to the people, and our covenant to God.

But there was a second way in which we came to understand the covenant. This was a new kind of blessing: a blessing of being-with. Naomi, widow of Bethlehem, lost both her sons in a time of famine. But one of her daughters-in-law, a Moabitess, insisted on remaining with her. She was called Ruth, and she exclaimed, 'Where you go, I will go; where you lodge, I will lodge; your people shall be my people, and your God my God. Where you die, I will die. Not even death will separate us.' Naomi's kinsman Boaz was moved by Ruth's faithfulness, and was kind to her. Boaz took Ruth as his wife. She bore Obed, whose son was Jesse.

One day old Samuel came to Bethlehem to see Jesse. Saul had lost favour in the Lord's sight: by sparing the king of Amalek after the Lord had given victory in battle, Saul had failed to trust and uphold the Lord's will. The Lord told Samuel, 'The Lord doesn't see as mortals see; they look on the outward appearance, but the Lord looks on the heart.' Jesse made seven of his sons pass before Samuel, and Samuel said to Jesse, 'The Lord has chosen none of these.' There remained yet the youngest, David, but he was keeping the sheep. When Samuel saw David, he took a horn of oil, and anointed him in front of his brothers; and the spirit of the Lord came mightily upon David.

Now we formed ranks against the Philistines. And out of

the camp of the Philistines came a champion named Goliath of Gath, who was a giant. He had a bronze helmet, and bronze armour that weighed 5,000 shekels. For 40 days, morning and evening, he shouted to us, 'Who will fight me?' And David heard him. David said to Saul, 'I will fight Goliath.' Saul said to David, 'You are just a boy.' But David said, 'The Lord, who saved me from the paw of the lion and from the paw of the bear, will save me from the hand of this Philistine.' So Saul clothed David with his armour. Then David said to Saul, 'I can't fight with these.' So he removed them. Then David chose five smooth stones from the wadi, put them in his shepherd's bag, and approached the Philistine. The Philistine despised David. But David said, 'You come to me with sword and spear and javelin; but I come to you in the name of the Lord of hosts, the God of the armies of Israel, whom you have defied.' David put his hand in his bag, took out a stone, slung it, and struck Goliath on his forehead; the stone sank into his forehead, and he fell down dead.

With David began a third notion of covenant – this time, of the lineage. Before any permanence could settle around the city, God promised through the prophet Nathan to make David a house. God said, 'I am the shepherd of the shepherd boy. I took you from following the sheep to be prince over my people Israel; and I have been with you wherever you went, and have cut off all your enemies from before you; and I will make for you a great name. And I will appoint a place for my people Israel; and I will give you rest from all your enemies. Your house and your throne shall be established for ever.'

Under David, Israel was no longer fending off the nations, living from crisis to disaster to restoration; now Israel was mighty, expanding, influential. Yet here was the paradox: God made David king not because he was handsome, but because he was pure in heart. David conquered not with great armour or power, but with wily sling and smooth stone. But David became like the mighty Goliath he had vanquished: and we did too. We had a new idea of covenant: to be a blessing by dominating other nations; to see God not in miracle, but in authority.

And this led to a fourth idea of covenant: the Temple. David had a magnificent palace in his new city of Jerusalem. But he reflected, 'I am living in a house of cedar, but the ark of God remains in a tent.' The two tablets of the Ten Commandments, whose presence in the midst of us meant God's dwelling place was with us, and whose periodic loss in battle to the Philistines was considered a catastrophe, had as yet no abiding place at our nation's heart. It fell to David's son Solomon to build a house for the Lord to shelter the ark of the covenant. In the four hundred and eightieth year after we came out of the land of Egypt, Solomon began to build the house of the Lord. He was seven years in building it.

He lined the internal walls with cedar; and he covered the floor with cypress. The inner sanctuary he overlaid with pure gold. He covered the whole house with gold, so that it might be perfect; even the altar of the inner sanctuary he covered with gold. In the inner sanctuary he made two cherubim of olive wood. He put the cherubim in the innermost part of the temple; the wings of the cherubim were spread out so that a wing of one was touching one wall, and a wing of the other was touching the other wall. He overlaid the cherubim with gold. The floor of the house he covered with gold. He covered the two doors of olive wood with carvings of cherubim, palm trees and open flowers; he overlaid them with gold, and spread gold on

the cherubim and on the palm trees. He made all the vessels –
the golden altar, the golden table for the bread of the Presence,
the lampstands of pure gold, in front of the inner sanctuary; the
flowers, the lamps and the tongs, cups, snuffers, basins, dishes
for incense, and firepans, of pure gold; the sockets for the doors
of the innermost part, the most holy place, and for the doors of
the nave of the temple, of gold.

Then the priests brought the ark of the covenant into the inner
sanctuary, the most holy place, underneath the wings of the
cherubim. And when the priests came out, a cloud filled the house
so that the priests couldn't stand; for the glory of the Lord filled the
Lord's house. Then Solomon wondered, 'Will God indeed dwell
on the earth? Even heaven and the highest heaven cannot contain
you, much less this house that I have built.' Yet he dedicated the
temple as a house where sin would be forgiven, and we would
pray for rain and success in battle. God would hear our pleas in
the face of famine, plague, blight, mildew, locust, caterpillar, and
the besieging of the enemy; and God would even hear the pleas of
the foreigner. Then Solomon sacrificed 22,000 oxen and 120,000
sheep, and held a festival for seven days.

This moment was the glory of our nation, its zenith. The
world looked on and the Queen of Sheba came from afar to pay
her respects. The covenant had borne fruit abundantly.

4

Fall

But something had already begun to go wrong. First David despised God, then David's family despised him. It was springtime, when kings go out to battle, but David remained at Jerusalem. David was walking about on the roof of the king's house. He saw from the roof a woman bathing; she was very beautiful. It was Bathsheba, the wife of Uriah the Hittite. So David sent for her. Afterwards she returned to her house. And she sent to tell David, 'I am pregnant.'

So David sent word to Joab his general, 'Send me Uriah the Hittite.' When Uriah came to him, David said to him, 'Go down to your house.' But Uriah slept at the entrance of the king's house and wouldn't go down to his house. Uriah said to David, 'The ark and Israel and Judah remain in booths; and Joab the general and the servants of my lord are camping in the open field; shall I then go to my house, to eat and to drink, and to lie with my wife?' So David wrote a letter to Joab, and sent it by the hand of Uriah. In the letter he wrote, 'Set Uriah in the forefront of the hardest fighting, and then draw back from him, so that he may be killed.' Then Joab sent and told David, 'Your servant Uriah the Hittite is dead.' David brought the wife of Uriah to his house, and she became his wife, and bore him a son.

The Lord sent Nathan to David, to say, 'There were two men

in a city, the one rich and the other poor. The rich man had very many flocks and herds; but the poor man had only one ewe lamb. It grew up with him and with his children; it used to eat of his meagre fare, and drink from his cup, and lie in his bosom, and it was like a daughter to him. Now there came a traveller to the rich man, and he was loath to take one of his own flock or herd to prepare for the wayfarer, but he took the poor man's lamb, and prepared that for his guest.' Then David was angry with the man. He said to Nathan, 'As the Lord lives, the man who has done this deserves to die; he shall restore the lamb fourfold, because he did this thing, and because he had no pity.' Nathan said to David, 'You are the man! The sword shall never depart from your house, for you have despised God.' David said to Nathan, 'I have sinned against the Lord.' On the seventh day the child died. Then David consoled his wife Bathsheba, and she bore a son, and he named him Solomon.

And it was like a second Fall. For in the mists of human beginnings, God had made Adam from the dust of the earth and had made Eve while Adam slept. God said, 'You may freely eat of every tree of the garden; but of the tree of the knowledge of good and evil you shall not eat.' But Adam and Eve took the abundance of plenty and saw only the scarcity of restraint. They jettisoned the joy of trust and purpose and substituted the anxiety of guilt and shame. Eve took the fruit and ate; and so did her husband. And they hid. And the Lord God came walking in the garden at the time of the evening breeze, and said, 'Where are you?' In just the same way, when their son Cain killed his brother Abel, the Lord said to Cain, 'Where is your brother?' David's fall from God's grace was followed in just the same way by the breakdown in his relationships.

Once rebellion had begun between the king and God, its poison seeped elsewhere. Absalom lost patience with his father's reluctance to uphold justice. Absalom stole our hearts. He proclaimed himself king. When the inevitable battle came, David said to his commanders, 'Deal gently for my sake with the young man Absalom.' 20,000 died. Absalom was riding on his mule as it went under the branches of a great oak. His hair caught fast in the oak, and he was left hanging between heaven and earth, while the mule that was under him went on. Joab took three spears and thrust them into Absalom's heart. Then Ahimaaz son of Zadok said, 'Let me run, and carry news to the king that the Lord has delivered him from the power of his enemies.' Joab said to him, 'You are not to carry news today.' Then Joab said to a Cushite, 'Go, tell the king what you have seen.' Then Ahimaaz ran by the way of the Plain, and outran the Cushite. Now David was sitting between the two gates. Then Ahimaaz cried out to the king, 'All is well!' He prostrated himself before the king with his face to the ground. The king said, 'Is it well with the young man Absalom?' Ahimaaz answered, 'When Joab sent your servant, I saw a great commotion, but I do not know what it was.' Then the Cushite came; and the Cushite said, 'Good news for my lord the king!' The king said to the Cushite, 'Is it well with the young man Absalom?' The Cushite answered, 'May the enemies of my lord the king, and all who rise up to do you harm, be like that young man.' The king was deeply moved, and went up to the chamber over the gate, and wept; and as he went, he said, 'O my son Absalom, my son, my son Absalom! Would I had died instead of you, O Absalom, my son, my son!'

5

Prophets

When Nathan spoke to the king and held up a mirror to what he was doing and had done, he demonstrated what prophecy meant and would come to mean for us. The prophet set the ways of the world against the ways of God, and showed how foolish and lost was the one if not lived in the light of the other.

Hosea expressed God's heart like this: 'When Israel was a child, I loved him, and out of Egypt I called my son. The more I called them, the more they went from me; they kept sacrificing to idols. Yet it was I who taught Ephraim to walk, I took them up in my arms; but they did not know that I healed them. I led them with cords of human kindness, with bands of love. I was to them like those who lift infants to their cheeks. I bent down to them and fed them. My people are bent on turning away from me. How can I give you up? How can I hand you over? My heart recoils within me; my compassion grows warm and tender. I will not execute my fierce anger; I will not again destroy my people; for I am God and no mortal, the Holy One in your midst, and I will not come in anger.'

Amos denounced all who failed to represent God in their dealings with the vulnerable. He said, 'Because you trample on the poor and push the afflicted out of the way, you have built houses of hewn stone, but you shall not live in them; you have planted pleasant vineyards, but you shall not drink their wine. For I know how great are your sins – you who afflict the righteous, who take a bribe, and push aside the needy in the gate. I hate your festivals, and take no delight in your solemn assemblies. Even though you offer me your burnt offerings and grain offerings, I will not accept them; and the offerings of your fatted animals I will not look upon. Take away from me the noise of your songs; I will not listen to the melody of your harps. But let justice roll down like waters, and righteousness like an ever-flowing stream.' And Micah added what God required when he asked, 'With what shall I come before the Lord, and bow myself before God on high? Shall I come before him with burnt offerings, with calves a year old? Will the Lord be pleased with thousands of rams, with 10,000 rivers of oil? Shall I give my firstborn for my transgression, the fruit of my body for the sin of my soul? He has told you what is good; and what does the Lord require of you but to do justice, and to love kindness, and to walk humbly with your God?'

The greatest of the prophets was Elijah. In his time the people were deserting the Lord God for the idols of Ba'al. He had all Israel assemble at Mount Carmel, with the 450 prophets of Ba'al. Elijah said, 'How long will you try to have it both ways? If the Lord is God, follow him; but if Ba'al, then follow him. Give me two bulls; let the prophets of Ba'al choose one bull for themselves, cut it in pieces, and lay it on the wood, but put no fire to it; I will prepare the other bull and lay it on the wood, but put no fire to it. Then you call on the name of your god and I will call on the name of the Lord; the god who answers by fire really is God.' So the prophets called on the name of Ba'al from morning until noon, crying, 'O Ba'al, answer us!' Elijah mocked, 'Is he meditating, or is he asleep?'

Then they cried aloud and cut themselves with swords and lances until the blood gushed out over them. Then Elijah said, 'Fill four jars with water and pour it on the burnt offering and on the wood.' Then he said, 'Do it a second time' and they did it a second time. Again he said, 'Do it a third time' and they did it a third time. Then he said, 'O Lord, God of Abraham, Isaac, and Israel, let everyone know that you are God in Israel.' Then the fire of the Lord fell and consumed the burnt offering, the wood, the stones, and the dust, and even licked up the water that was in the trench. Elijah seized the prophets of Ba'al, brought them down to the Wadi Kishon, and slaughtered them there.

That sin, that fall, which David embodied, Amos lamented and Elijah confronted, had been there from the beginning. Amos describes half of sin, the blasphemy of failing to recognize one's brother and sister as the image of God. Elijah attacks the other half of sin, the idolatry of turning aside from God and instead worshipping something more congenial. When Moses was on Mount Sinai with God, we all gathered around his brother Aaron, and said, 'Make gods for us.' We all took off our gold earrings and brought them to Aaron. He took the gold from them, formed it in a mould, and cast an image of a calf, and said, 'These are your gods, O Israel, who brought you up out of the land of Egypt!' The Lord said to Moses, 'I have seen how stiff-necked this people are. Now let me alone, so that my anger may burn hot against them.' But Moses implored the Lord God, and said, 'Turn from your fierce anger; change your mind and don't bring disaster on your people.' And the Lord did have a change of mind.

Our life was guided by the offices of prophet, priest and king. When Elijah's time was drawing to an end, Elijah said to

Elisha, 'Stay here; for the Lord has sent me as far as Bethel.' But Elisha said, 'As the Lord lives, and as you yourself live, I will not leave you.' Elijah said to him, 'Elisha, stay here; for the Lord has sent me to Jericho.' But he said, 'As the Lord lives, and as you yourself live, I will not leave you.' So they came to Jericho. Then Elijah said to him, 'Stay here; for the Lord has sent me to the Jordan.' But he said, 'As the Lord lives, and as you yourself live, I will not leave you.' Then Elijah took his mantle and rolled it up, and struck the water; the water was parted, until the two of them crossed on dry ground. Elisha said, 'Let me inherit a double share of your spirit.' As they continued walking and talking, a chariot of fire and horses of fire separated them, and Elijah ascended in a whirlwind into heaven. Elisha kept watching and crying out, 'Father, father! The chariots of Israel and its horsemen!' He took the mantle of Elijah that had fallen from him, and struck the water, saying, 'Where is the Lord, the God of Elijah?' When he had struck the water, the water was parted, and Elisha went over. When the company of prophets who were at Jericho saw him at a distance, they declared, 'The spirit of Elijah rests on Elisha.' Thus did God's guiding hand stay with us.

Not all the kings were wayward and not always were we faithless. King Josiah found a book of the law that had been forgotten for generations. He read to all the inhabitants of Jerusalem the words of the book of the covenant. He deposed the idolatrous priests, burned the vessels made for Ba'al, broke down the houses of the temple prostitutes, burned the chariots of the sun, slaughtered on their altars all the priests of the high places in Samaria, and kept the first Passover since the days of the judges. Before him there was no king like him, who turned to the Lord with all his heart, with all his soul, and with all his might, according to all the law of Moses; nor did any like him arise after him. One of the greatest of our songs goes, 'Oh, how I love your law! It is my meditation all day long. How sweet are your words to my taste, sweeter than honey to my mouth! Your word is a lamp to my feet and a light to my path.'

6

Exile

When it all ended it was savage and blunt. The king of Assyria invaded all the land and came to Samaria; for three years he besieged it. Then he captured Samaria; he carried the Israelites of the ten northern tribes away to Assyria. Those ten northern tribes of Israel never returned. One hundred and forty years later King Nebuchadnezzar of Babylon came with all his army against Jerusalem, and laid siege to it. The famine became so severe that there was no food for the people of the city. Then a breach was made in the city wall; King Zedekiah and all his soldiers fled by night. But the army of the Chaldeans overtook him in the plains of Jericho. All his army was scattered, deserting him. They slaughtered his sons before his eyes, and put out his eyes; they bound him in fetters and took him to Babylon. The Chaldeans burned the house of the Lord, the king's house, all the houses of Jerusalem, and broke down the walls around Jerusalem. They carried into exile those of us who were left in the city and the deserters who had defected to the king of Babylon – all the rest of the population. But the captain of the guard left some of the poorest people of the land to be vinedressers and tillers of the soil. So the remaining two southern tribes of Judah went into exile out of our land.

Desperate was our dismay. This is how we lamented: 'How

lonely sits the city that once was full of people! How like a widow she has become, she that was great among the nations! Judah has gone into exile with suffering and hard servitude; she lives now among the nations, and finds no resting place. The Lord has made her suffer for the multitude of her transgressions. Is it nothing to you, all you who pass by? Look and see if there is any sorrow like my sorrow. The Lord has trodden as in a wine press the virgin daughter Judah. See, Lord, how distressed I am; my stomach churns, my heart is wrung within me, because I have been very rebellious. My groans are many and my heart is faint.'

By the rivers of Babylon – there we sat down and there we wept when we remembered Zion. On the willows there we hung up our harps. For there our captors asked us for songs, and our tormentors laughed, saying, 'Sing us one of the songs of Zion!' But how could we sing the Lord's song in a foreign land?

Was this the way our story with God would end? We searched the soul of God. We said, 'O Lord, you search me and you know me. You are acquainted with all my ways. Even before a word is on my tongue, O Lord, you know it completely. Such knowledge is too wonderful for me. Where can I go from your spirit? Or where can I flee from your presence? Even the darkness is not dark to you; the night is as bright as the day, for darkness is as light to you. In your book were written all the days that were formed for me, when none of them as yet existed. How weighty to me are your thoughts, O God! How vast is the sum of them! I try to count them – they are more than the sand; I come to the end – I am still with you.'

Surely this God was not finished with us yet. This was when we wrote down our story. This is where, in a way, our story really began. This was when we began to discover who God really is. Nebuchadnezzar thought he was the end of our story. But in the fire, we found that God was with us.

7

Renewal

And indeed things began to change. There was a letter. The prophet Jeremiah wrote from Jerusalem to the exiles. He said, 'Build houses and live in them; plant gardens and eat what they produce. Take wives and have sons and daughters; take wives for your sons, and give your daughters in marriage, that they may bear sons and daughters; multiply there, and do not decrease. But seek the welfare of the city where you have been sent into exile, and pray to the Lord on its behalf, for in its welfare you will find your welfare. Thus says the Lord, "Only when Babylon's 70 years are completed will I visit you, and I will fulfil my promise and bring you back to this place. For surely I know the plans I have for you, plans for your welfare and not for harm, to give you a future with hope. Then when you call upon me and come and pray to me, I will hear you. When you search for me, you will find me; if you seek me with all your heart, I will let you find me, and I will restore your fortunes and gather you from all the nations and all the places where I have driven you, and I will bring you back to the place from which I sent you into exile."'

Then there was a vision. Even in the heat of the fire, God was with us. Isaiah showed us God's purpose in these words: 'Thus says the Lord, who created you, O Jacob, who formed you, O Israel: "Do not fear, for I have redeemed you; I have called you by name, you are mine. When you pass through the waters, I'll be with you; and through the rivers, they shall not overwhelm you; when you walk through fire you shall not be burned, and the flame shall not consume you. For I am the Lord your God, the Holy One of Israel, your Saviour. I give Egypt as your ransom, Ethiopia and Seba in exchange for you. Because you are precious in my sight, and honoured, and I love you, I give people in return for you, nations in exchange for your life. Do not fear, for I am with you; I will bring your offspring from the east, and from the west I will gather you; I will say to the north, 'Give them up,' and to the south, 'Do not withhold; bring my sons from far away and my daughters from the end of the earth – everyone who is called by my name, whom I created for my glory, whom I formed and made.'"' In exile, we were yet precious, honoured, and loved.

Meanwhile Jeremiah was given moments of clarity and understanding. The Lord said, 'Go down to the potter's house.' The vessel the potter was making of clay was spoiled in the potter's hand, and he reworked it into another vessel, as seemed good to him. Then the word of the Lord came to Jeremiah: 'Can I not do with you, O house of Israel, just as this potter has done?' And even before Jerusalem had been destroyed Jeremiah had realized it was the will of the Lord for him to go and buy a field at Anathoth, regardless of the besieging Chaldean armies. For the Lord was saying, 'Houses and fields and vineyards shall again be bought in this land.'

Then there was a new revelation of God. The exile was not just grief for us; it was untold suffering for God. Isaiah again saw what was happening: 'He had no form or majesty that we should look at him, nothing in his appearance that we should desire him. He was despised and rejected by others; a man of suffering and acquainted with infirmity; and as one from whom others hide their faces he was despised, and we held him of no account. Surely he has borne our infirmities and carried our diseases. But he was wounded for our transgressions, crushed for our iniquities; upon him was the punishment that made us whole, and by his bruises we are healed. He was oppressed, and he was afflicted, yet he did not open his mouth; like a lamb that is led to the slaughter, and like a sheep that before its shearers is silent, so he did not open his mouth.'

And then through Ezekiel there was given hope for the resurrection of our people. 'The Lord brought me out by the spirit and set me down in the middle of a valley full of dry bones. He said to me, "Can these bones live?" Thus says the Lord God to these bones: "I will cause breath to enter you, and you shall live. I will lay sinews on you, and will cause flesh to come upon you, and cover you with skin, and put breath in you, and you shall live; and you shall know that I am the Lord." And as I prophesied, suddenly there was a noise, a rattling, and the bones came together, bone to its bone. I looked, and there were sinews on them, and flesh had come upon them, and skin had covered them; but there was no breath in them. Then he said to me, "Prophesy to the breath: Come from the four winds, O breath, and breathe upon these slain, that they may live." The breath came into them, and they lived, and stood on their feet, a vast multitude. Then he said to me, "These bones are the whole house of Israel. They say, 'Our bones are dried up, and our hope is lost; we are cut off completely.'" Thus says the Lord God: "I am going to open your graves, and bring you up from your graves, O my people; and I will bring you back to the land of Israel. I will put my spirit within you, and you shall live, and I will place you on your own soil."'

At this moment Isaiah proclaimed, "'Comfort my people," says your God. "Speak tenderly to Jerusalem, and cry to her that she has served her term, that her penalty is paid, that she has received from the Lord's hand double for all her sins. Make straight in the desert a highway for our God. Every valley shall be lifted up, and every mountain and hill be made low; the uneven ground shall become level, and the rough places a plain. Then the glory of the Lord shall be revealed, and all people shall see it together, for the mouth of the Lord has spoken."'

And Jeremiah said, 'The days are coming, says the Lord, when I will make a new covenant with the house of Israel and the house of Judah. It will not be like the covenant that I made with their ancestors when I took them by the hand to bring them out of the land of Egypt. I will put my law within them, and I will write it on their hearts; and I will be their God, and they shall be my people. They shall all know me, from the least of them to the greatest; for I will forgive their iniquity, and remember their sin no more.'

And it came to pass. When the empire of Babylon had been defeated by Persia, the Lord stirred up King Cyrus of Persia so that he declared: 'The Lord, the God of heaven has given me all the kingdoms of the earth, and he has charged me to build him a house at Jerusalem in Judah. Any of those among you who are of his people – may their God be with them! – are now permitted to go up to Jerusalem in Judah, and rebuild the house of the Lord, the God of Israel – the God who is in Jerusalem; and let all survivors, in whatever place they reside, be assisted by the people of their place with silver and gold, with goods and with animals, besides freewill offerings for the house of God in Jerusalem.' And so it was. And later King Artaxerxes sent Nehemiah to rebuild the fortifications of Jerusalem, giving him timber to make beams for the gates of the temple fortress, and for the wall of the city.

8

Return

Then we sang together, 'When the Lord restored the fortunes of Zion, we were like those who dream. Our mouth was filled with laughter, and our tongue with shouts of joy; then it was said among the nations, "The Lord has done great things for them." May those who sow in tears reap with shouts of joy.' And Isaiah said, 'You shall go out in joy, and be led back in peace; the mountains and the hills before you shall burst into song, and all the trees of the field shall clap their hands. Instead of the thorn shall come up the cypress; instead of the brier shall come up the myrtle; and it shall be to the Lord for a memorial, for an everlasting sign that shall not be cut off.' Lovers said to one another, 'Now the winter is past, the rain is over and gone. The flowers appear on the earth; the time of singing has come, and the voice of the turtledove is heard in our land. Many waters cannot quench love; neither can floods overcome it. For love is strong as death.' And the prophet Joel said, 'O children of Zion, I will restore to you the years that the swarming locust has eaten. And my people shall never again be put to shame.' And the poet Job said, 'I know that my Redeemer lives, and that at the last he will stand upon the earth; and after my skin has been thus destroyed, then in my flesh I shall see God, whom I shall see on my side, and my eyes shall behold, and not another.'

But not all of us came home. And one, Esther, became Queen of Persia. When our enemies looked set to obliterate us all from across the empire, Esther realized that she had come to royal dignity for just such a time as this. She persuaded King Ahasuerus to overturn the decree and our people avoided extermination by the thread of her faithful courage.

In exile we had discovered who we truly were and who God truly was. We knew some things like never before. We discovered that 'The steadfast love of the Lord never ceases. Your mercies never come to an end; they are new every morning; great is your faithfulness. The Lord will not reject forever. Although God causes grief, it comes with compassion according to the abundance of steadfast love; for the Lord does not willingly afflict or grieve anyone.'

And after our return we found a new hope for our people. We said, 'The spirit of the Lord God is upon us, because the Lord has anointed us; he has sent us to bring good news to the oppressed, to bind up the broken-hearted, to proclaim liberty to the captives, and release to the prisoners; to proclaim the year of the Lord's favour, and the day of vengeance of our God; to comfort all who mourn; to give them a garland instead of ashes, the oil of gladness instead of mourning, the mantle of praise instead of a faint spirit. We shall build up the ancient ruins, we shall raise up the former devastations; we shall repair the ruined cities, the devastations of many generations. We shall be called priests of the Lord, we shall enjoy the wealth of the nations, and in their riches we shall glory. Because our shame was double, and dishonour was proclaimed as our lot, therefore we shall possess a double portion; everlasting joy shall be ours.'

We had a vision of a reign of justice and well-being, which we called shalom. Isaiah foresaw God's purposes: 'For I am about to create new heavens and a new earth. I am about to create Jerusalem as a joy, and its people as a delight. I will rejoice in Jerusalem, and delight in my people; no more shall the sound of weeping be heard in it, or the cry of distress. They shall build houses and inhabit them; they shall plant vineyards and eat their fruit. The wolf and the lamb shall feed together, the lion shall eat straw like the ox. They shall not hurt or destroy on all my holy mountain, says the Lord.'

And as we looked back we saw the Lord had been our shepherd, and had led us through green pastures and beside still waters. The Lord had restored our soul. Even though we had walked through the darkest valley, we would no longer fear evil; for the Lord had been with us, had spread a table before us in the presence of our enemies, and anointed our head with oil; our cup overflowed. Surely, we said, goodness and mercy shall follow us all the days of our life, and we shall dwell in the house of the Lord for ever.

Part Two

9

Resurrection

Paul was in a different kind of exile: he was in Rome. He believed he had done nothing against our people, yet he'd been arrested in Jerusalem and handed over to the Romans. The Romans wanted to release him; but our own people objected. So, being a Roman citizen, he appealed to the emperor. And that brought him to Rome. Was he truly a loyal citizen of the emperor? Was he truly a faithful Jew? Or were both Jews and Romans right to perceive this was something new, subversive, and threatening?

Surely what happened at Easter answered those questions. Jesus had been crucified, asphyxiated, and a spear had been thrust through his heart. Joseph of Arimathea had provided a tomb in which no one had previously been laid. But early on the third day Mary Magdalene and other women had come to the tomb and seen that the stone had been rolled away. Mary ran and told Peter and the beloved disciple, 'They have taken the Lord away.' Peter came and went into the tomb. The other disciple, who reached the tomb first, also went in, and saw the linen wrappings lying there, and believed. But Mary remained outside the tomb, weeping. As she wept, she saw two angels in white, sitting where the body of Jesus had been lying, one at the head and the other at the feet. They said to her, 'Woman, why are you weeping?' She said to them, 'They have taken away my

Lord.' When she had said this, she turned round and saw Jesus standing there, but she did not know that it was Jesus. Jesus said to her, 'Why are you weeping? For whom are you looking?' Then he said, 'Mary!' She turned and said, 'Teacher.' Mary went and announced to the disciples, 'I have seen the Lord.'

That night, despite the locked doors, Jesus came and stood among the disciples and said, 'Peace be with you.' Then he showed them his hands and his side. But Thomas was not with them. He said to them, 'Unless I see and put my finger in the mark of the nails, I will not believe.' A week later Jesus again came and stood among them. Then he said to Thomas, 'Put your finger here and see my hands and my side. Do not doubt but believe.' Thomas answered him, 'My Lord and my God!'

What Mary Magdalene saw was a new mercy seat, a new ark of the covenant with angels at head and foot, a new place of reconciliation between us and God. The risen Jesus had become the new temple. And what Thomas proclaimed; My Lord and My God was the vainglorious title of the Roman emperor, My Lord and my God, now assigned to Jesus, the risen Lord of heaven and earth. In his resurrection, Jesus was overturning both the Roman and the Jewish understanding of present, past and future, God and humanity, authority and salvation.

On the evening of Easter Day two disciples were going to a village called Emmaus. While they were talking, Jesus himself came alongside, and said, 'What are you discussing?' They stood still, looking sad. Then one answered, 'Are you the only stranger in Jerusalem who doesn't know about Jesus of Nazareth, and how our chief priests and leaders handed him over to be condemned to death and crucified him? Some women of our group astounded us. They found his tomb empty, and told us that they had seen angels who said that he was alive.' Then Jesus said, 'How foolish you are, and slow to believe. Was it not necessary that the Messiah should suffer these things and then enter into his glory?' He walked ahead, but they urged him, 'Stay with us.' When he was at the table with them, he took bread, blessed and broke it, and gave it to them. Then their eyes were opened, and they recognized him; and he vanished from their sight.

One night seven of the disciples went fishing on the Sea of Galilee, but caught nothing. Just after daybreak, Jesus stood on the beach. He said, 'Cast the net to the right side of the boat.' And they caught 153 fish, and they weren't able to haul in the net. Jesus was saying if they were exhausted spreading the gospel to the Jews, it was time to bring the good news to the nations, where there would be too many adherents to comprehend or contain.

In Galilee, Jesus met eleven disciples on a mountain and said to them, 'All authority in heaven and on earth has been given to me. Go and make disciples of all nations, baptizing them in the name of the Father and of the Son and of the Holy Spirit, and teaching them to obey everything that I have commanded you. And remember, I am with you always.'

10

Incarnation

Who was this Jesus whom God so raised from the dead?

The angel Gabriel came to Mary of Nazareth and said, 'You are favoured. The Lord is with you. You will conceive and bear a son, and you will name him Jesus. His kingdom is forever.' Mary said, 'How can this be? I am a virgin.' The angel said to her, 'The Holy Spirit will come upon you. The child to be born will be called Son of God. Nothing is impossible with God.' Then Mary said, 'I am the servant of the Lord; let it be with me according to your word.' When Mary greeted her kinswoman Elizabeth, she sang, 'The Mighty One has done great things for me. The Lord has scattered the proud in the thoughts of their hearts, brought down the powerful from their thrones, and lifted up the lowly; filled the hungry with good things, and sent the rich away empty.'

The coming of Jesus reassembled the Old Testament story. Jesus came among us to change, restore, and transform; and the prophets' ministry was alive in him. Israel was favoured like in the time of David, and we hear again the words 'for ever'. Jesus is to be holy, a return to the promise of Moses of a holy nation. Shortly he would spend 40 days in the wilderness, as Moses spent 40 years. He stood in the line of the house of Jacob, his 12 disciples re-inhabited the legacy of the 12 tribes, he reinvoked the call of Abraham to be a blessing to the nations. As the servant of the Lord, Mary dwelt in God's house day and night, and by saying 'Let it be', in being subject to God's word and in the Spirit hovering over her, she became a whole new creation story. This was about a new genesis, a second beginning of all things.

Mary's betrothed was Joseph. Joseph was the fourteenth generation since the exile, and there were 14 generations from the exile back to Joseph's ancestor David. And there were 14 generations from David back to Abraham. When Mary was found to be with child, an angel of the Lord appeared to Joseph in a dream and said, 'Joseph, take Mary as your wife, for the child is from the Holy Spirit. She will bear a son, and you are to name him Jesus, for he will save his people from their sins.' As the prophet foretold, 'The virgin shall conceive and bear a son, and they shall name him Emmanuel', which means, 'God is with us.'

But this story was not just about humanity or Israel. For the Word was in the beginning and the Word was with God, bringing all things into being. The Word was coming into the world. The world came into being through him; yet the world did not accept him. The Word became flesh and lived among us, and we have seen his glory, the glory as of a father's only son, full of grace and truth. The law was indeed given through Moses; grace and truth came through Jesus Christ. God the only Son, who is close to the Father's heart, made God known like never before.

Since he was descended from David, Joseph took his wife to be registered for the great census in Bethlehem. While they were there, Mary gave birth and wrapped her son in bands of cloth, and laid him in a manger, because there was no place for them in the inn. An angel of the Lord appeared to shepherds and said to them, 'To you is born this day in the city of David a Saviour, who is the Messiah, the Lord.' Suddenly there was with the angel a multitude of the heavenly host singing, 'Glory in heaven, peace on earth.'

11

Teaching

Isaiah had said to God, 'O that you would tear open the heavens and come down'; and at the Jordan it happened. Jesus came from Galilee to be baptized by John the Baptist. And just as he came up from the water, the heavens were torn asunder and he saw the Spirit of God descending like a dove and alighting on him. And a voice from heaven said, 'This is my Son, the Beloved, with whom I am well pleased.' This was the new Joshua crossing over into the new Promised Land as precious, honoured and loved as Isaiah had affirmed.

And just as Israel had gone from liberation into wilderness, so Jesus went straightaway from baptism to the desert. The tempter came and said, 'If you are the Son of God, command these stones to become loaves of bread.' But he answered, 'We live not by bread alone, but by the word of God.' Then the devil said, 'If you are the Son of God, throw yourself down from the pinnacle of the temple.' Jesus replied, 'Do not put the Lord your God to the test.' The devil showed him all the kingdoms of the world and promised, 'All these I will give you, if you will fall down and worship me.' Jesus said to him, 'Worship and serve the Lord your God alone.'

Just as Israel had 12 tribes, Jesus called 12 disciples. As he walked by the Sea of Galilee, he saw Simon Peter and Andrew his brother, casting a net into the lake. And he said, 'Follow me, and I will make you fish for people.' Immediately they left their nets and followed him. He saw James and his brother John in the boat with their father Zebedee, mending their nets, and he called them. Immediately they left the boat and their father, and followed him. There were also Philip and Bartholomew, Thomas and Matthew the tax-collector, James son of Alphaeus, Thaddaeus, Simon the Zealot, and Judas Iscariot. He instructed them, 'Proclaim the good news, "The kingdom of heaven has come near." Cure the sick, raise the dead, cleanse lepers, cast out demons. Take no gold, or silver, or copper in your belts, no bag for your journey, or two tunics, or sandals, or a staff. If anyone will not welcome you or listen to your words, shake off the dust from your feet as you leave that house or town. I am sending you out like sheep into the midst of wolves; so be wise as serpents and innocent as doves. Whoever loves father or mother more than me is not worthy of me; and whoever loves son or daughter more than me is not worthy of me; and whoever does not take up the cross and follow me is not worthy of me. Those who find their life will lose it, and those who lose their life for my sake will find it.'

Jesus taught the disciples and the crowds. Like Moses he stood on a mountain, and said, 'Blessed are the poor in spirit, for theirs is the kingdom of heaven. Blessed are those who mourn, for they will be comforted. Blessed are the meek, for they will inherit the earth. Blessed are those who hunger and thirst for righteousness, for they will be filled. Blessed are the merciful, for they will receive mercy. Blessed are the pure in heart, for they will see God. Blessed are the peacemakers, for they will be called children of God. Blessed are those who are persecuted for righteousness' sake, for theirs is the kingdom of heaven.

'You were told, "You shall not murder"; but do not be angry. You were told, "You shall not commit adultery." But I say, "Do not lust." You were told, "You shall not swear falsely." But I say, "Do not swear at all." You were told, "An eye for an eye and a tooth for a tooth." But I say to you, "Do not resist an evildoer." You were told, "You shall love your neighbour and hate your enemy." But I say to you, "Love your enemies and pray for those who persecute you." Be perfect, as your heavenly Father is perfect.

'When you give alms, do not let your left hand know what your right hand is doing. When you fast, put oil on your head and wash your face, so that your fasting may be seen not by others but by your Father who is in secret. When you pray, go into your room and shut the door and pray to your Father who is in secret. Pray in this way: Our Father in heaven, hallowed be your name. Your kingdom come. Your will be done, on earth as it is in heaven. Give us this day our daily bread. And forgive us our debts, as we also have forgiven our debtors. And do not bring us to the time of trial, but rescue us from the evil one.

'Don't worry about what you will eat or drink or wear. The birds of the air neither sow nor reap nor gather into barns, yet your heavenly Father feeds them. Consider the lilies of the field, how they grow; they neither toil nor spin, yet I tell you, even Solomon in all his glory was not clothed like one of these. But if God so clothes the grass of the field, which is alive today and tomorrow is thrown into the oven, will he not much more clothe you – you of little faith? Strive first for the kingdom of God, and all these things will be given to you as well.

'Do not judge, so that you may not be judged. Why do you see the speck in your neighbour's eye, but do not notice the log in your own eye? Or how can you say to your neighbour, "Let me take the speck out of your eye", while the log is in your own eye? You hypocrite, first take the log out of your own eye, and then you will see clearly to take the speck out of your neighbour's eye. Ask, and it will be given to you; search, and you will find; knock, and the door will be opened for you. In everything do to others as you would have them do to you; for this is the law and the prophets.'

One of the scribes asked Jesus, 'Which commandment is the first of all?' Jesus answered, 'The first is, "You shall love the Lord your God with all your heart, and with all your soul, and with all your mind, and with all your strength." The second is this, "You shall love your neighbour as yourself." There is no other commandment greater than these.'

12

Parables

Jesus taught many things in parables. He said, 'A man was going down from Jerusalem to Jericho, and fell into the hands of robbers, who stripped him, beat him, and went away, leaving him half dead. Now a priest was going down that road; and when he saw him, he passed by on the other side. So likewise did a Levite. But a Samaritan came near and was moved with pity. He went to him and bandaged his wounds. Then he brought him to an inn, and took care of him. The next day he said to the innkeeper, "Take care of him; and when I come back, I will repay you whatever more you spend." Go and do likewise.'

Again, 'A man had two sons. The younger said, "Father, give me the share of the property that will belong to me." So he divided his property. That son travelled to a distant country, and there squandered his property in dissolute living. A severe famine took hold, so he hired himself out to a local farmer, who sent him to feed his pigs. When he came to himself he said, "How many of my father's hired hands have bread to spare, but here I am dying of hunger! I will go to my father, and say to him, 'Treat me like one of your hired hands.'" But while he was still far off, his father saw him. He was filled with compassion. Running out he put his arms around his son and kissed him. Then the son said, "Father, I have sinned against heaven and before you; I am no longer worthy to be called your son." But the father said to his slaves, "Quickly, bring out the best robe and put it on him; put a ring on his finger and sandals on his feet. Kill the fatted calf, and let us eat and celebrate; for this son of mine was dead and is alive again; he was lost and is found." And they began to celebrate.

'Now his elder son was in the field; and he heard music and dancing. He called one of the slaves who said, "Your brother has come, and your father has killed the fatted calf, because he has got him back safe and sound." Then he became angry and refused to go in. His father came out to plead with him. But he answered, "Listen! All these years I have slaved for you. I have never disobeyed your command. Yet you have never given me even a young goat so that I might celebrate with my friends. But when this son of yours came back, after devouring your property with prostitutes, you killed the fatted calf for him!" Then the father said to him, "Son, you are always with me, and all that is mine is yours. But we had to celebrate and rejoice, because this brother of yours was dead and has come to life; he was lost and has been found."'

Again, 'The kingdom of heaven is like a landowner who went out early in the morning to hire labourers for his vineyard. He agreed with the labourers for the usual daily wage, and sent them into his vineyard. About nine o'clock, he saw others standing idle in the marketplace; and he said to them, "You also go into the vineyard, and I will pay you whatever is right." So they went. When he went out again about noon and about three o'clock, he did the same. About five o'clock he went out and found others standing around. He said to them, "You also go into the vineyard." When evening came, the owner of the vineyard said to his manager, "Call the labourers and give them their pay, beginning with the last and then going to the first." When those hired about five o'clock came, each of them received the usual daily wage. Now when the first came, they thought they would receive more; but each of them also received the usual daily wage. And they grumbled against the landowner. But he replied to one of them, "Am I not allowed to do what I choose with what belongs to me? Or are you envious because I am generous?"'

Again, 'The kingdom of heaven is like a merchant in search of fine pearls; on finding one pearl of great value, he went and sold all that he had and bought it.' Again, 'A man gave a great dinner and invited many. But they all alike began to make excuses. "I have bought a piece of land." "I have bought five yoke of oxen." "I have just been married." Then the host said to his slave, "Go out at once into the streets and lanes of the town and bring in the poor, the crippled, the blind, and the lame. For I tell you, none of those who were invited will taste my dinner."'

And he described how he will judge us by how we have judged him. 'When the Son of Man comes in his glory, and all the angels with him, he will separate people one from another as a shepherd separates the sheep from the goats, and he will put the sheep at his right hand and the goats at the left. Then the king will say to those at his right hand, "Come, you that are blessed by my Father, inherit the kingdom prepared for you from the foundation of the world; for I was hungry and you gave me food, I was thirsty and you gave me something to drink, I was a stranger and you welcomed me, I was naked and you gave me clothing, I was sick and you took care of me, I was in prison and you visited me." Then the righteous will answer him, "Lord, when was it that we saw you hungry and gave you food, or thirsty and gave you something to drink? And when was it that we saw you a stranger and welcomed you, or naked and gave you clothing? And when was it that we saw you sick or in prison and visited you?" And the king will answer them, "Truly I tell you, just as you did it to one of the least of these who are members of my family, you did it to me.'"

In seven ways Jesus declared who he was. He said, 'I am the bread of life. Whoever comes to me will never be hungry, and whoever believes in me will never be thirsty. I am the light of the world. Whoever follows me will never walk in darkness but will have the light of life. I am the gate for the sheep. Whoever enters by me will be saved. I came that they may have life, and have it abundantly. I am the good shepherd. The good shepherd lays down his life for the sheep. I am the resurrection and the life. Those who believe in me, even though they die, will live, and everyone who lives and believes in me will never die. I am the way, and the truth, and the life. No one comes to the Father except through me. I am the true vine; abide in me.'

God loved the world. God's love was so great as to say, 'I am sending my only Son.' Everyone who believes in the Son will not perish but have eternal life.

13

Miracles

Jesus demonstrated God in actions even more than he revealed the kingdom in words. When he was in Capernaum, so many gathered that there was no room for them. Then some people came, bringing to him a paralysed man, carried by four of them. And they removed the roof above him; and after having dug through it, they let down the mat on which the paralytic lay. When Jesus saw their faith, he said to the paralytic, 'Son, your sins are forgiven.' Now some of the scribes were sitting there, questioning in their hearts, 'Who can forgive sins but God alone?' Jesus said, 'Which is easier, to say to the paralytic, "Your sins are forgiven", or to say, "Stand up and take your mat and walk"? But so that you may know that the Son of Man has authority on earth to forgive sins' – he said to the paralytic – 'I say to you, stand up, take your mat and go to your home.' And he stood up, and immediately took the mat and went out before all of them. It was like Israel overcoming paralysis and standing on its own two feet again.

Once Jesus taught a great crowd. When it grew late, his disciples protested that the people were hungry. He said, 'How many loaves have you?' They said, 'Five, and two fish.' Taking the five loaves and the two fish, he looked up to heaven, and blessed and broke the loaves, and gave them to his disciples to set before the people; and he divided the two fish among them all. And all ate and were filled; and they took up 12 baskets full of broken pieces and of the fish. Those who had eaten numbered 5,000. It was like the scarcity of fallen humankind turning into the abundance of the kingdom of God.

Once Jesus made the disciples get into a boat and cross the Sea of Galilee, while he went up the mountain to pray. When evening came, the boat, battered by the waves, was far from the land, for the wind was against them. And early in the morning he came walking towards them on the lake. But when the disciples saw him walking on the lake, they were terrified. And they cried out in fear. But Jesus spoke to them and said, 'Take heart, it is I; do not be afraid.' Peter answered him, 'Lord, if it is you, command me to come to you on the water.' He said, 'Come.' So Peter got out of the boat, started walking on the water, and came towards Jesus. But when he noticed the strong wind, he became frightened, and beginning to sink, he cried out, 'Lord, save me!' Jesus immediately reached out his hand and caught him, saying to him, 'You of little faith, why did you doubt?' When they got into the boat, the wind ceased. And those in the boat worshipped him, saying, 'Truly you are the Son of God.'

On the other side of the sea was the country of the Gerasenes. When Jesus stepped out of the boat, a man with an unclean spirit stepped forward. No one had the strength to subdue him. Night and day among the tombs and on the mountains he was always howling and bruising himself with stones. When he saw Jesus from a distance, he ran and bowed down before him; and he shouted at the top of his voice, 'What have you to do with me, Jesus, Son of the Most High God? By God, do not torment me.' For he had said to the man, 'Come out, you unclean spirit!' Then Jesus asked the man, 'What is your name?' He replied, 'My name is Legion; for we are many.' He begged him earnestly not to send them out of the country. Now there on the hillside a great herd of swine was feeding and the unclean spirits begged him, 'Send us into the swine; let us enter them.' So he gave them permission. And the unclean spirits came out and entered the swine; and the herd, numbering about 2,000, rushed down the steep bank into the sea, and were drowned in the sea. Then people saw the demoniac sitting there, clothed and in his right mind, the very man who had had the legion and they were afraid. And it was like the Roman legions and their unclean pigs were being cleansed from Israel.

Jesus went to the villages of Caesarea Philippi; and on the way he asked his disciples, 'Who do people say that I am?' And they answered, 'John the Baptist; and others, Elijah; and still others, one of the prophets.' He asked them, 'But who do you say that I am?' Peter answered him, 'You are the Messiah.' And he sternly ordered them not to tell anyone about him. Then he began to teach them that the Son of Man must undergo great suffering, and be rejected by the elders, the chief priests, and the scribes, and be killed, and after three days rise again. He called the crowd and said to them, 'If any want to become my followers, let them deny themselves and take up their cross and follow me. For those who want to save their life will lose it, and those who lose their life for my sake, and for the sake of the gospel, will save it. For what will it profit them to gain the whole world and forfeit their life?' And it was like Jesus was saying he was going to lose his life and so gain the whole world.

Six days later, Jesus took with him Peter and James and John, and led them up a high mountain apart, by themselves. And he was transfigured before them, and his clothes became dazzling white. And Elijah and Moses appeared to them, talking with Jesus. Then Peter said, 'Rabbi, it is good for us to be here; let us make three dwellings, one for you, one for Moses, and one for Elijah.' He did not know what to say, they were so terrified. Then a cloud overshadowed them, and from the cloud there came a voice, 'This is my Son, the Beloved; listen to him!' Suddenly when they looked around, they saw no one with them anymore, but only Jesus. And it was like the law of Moses and the prophetic witness of Elijah had both been fulfilled in this one person.

James and John said to him, 'Teacher, grant us to sit, one at your right hand and one at your left, in your glory.' But Jesus said to them, 'You know that among the Gentiles their rulers lord it over them. But it is not so among you; but whoever wishes to become great among you must be your servant, and whoever wishes to be first among you must be slave of all. For the Son of Man came not to be served but to serve, and to give his life a ransom for many.'

Jesus' friend Lazarus became ill. Jesus said to the disciples, 'Let us go to Judea.' The disciples said to him, 'Rabbi, the Jews were just now trying to stone you, and are you going there again?' Thomas said, 'Let us go, that we may die with him.' When Jesus arrived, Lazarus had already been in the tomb for four days. Lazarus' sister Martha said to Jesus, 'Lord, if you had been here, my brother would not have died.' Jesus said, 'Your brother will rise again.' Martha said, 'You are the Messiah, the Son of God, the one coming into the world.' Jesus said, 'Where have you laid him?' Jesus wept. So the Jews said, 'See how he loved him!' Then Jesus came to the tomb. He said, 'Take away the stone.' Martha said, 'Lord, there is a stench because he has been dead four days.' Jesus said to her, 'Did I not tell you that if you believed, you would see the glory of God?' So they took away the stone. Jesus looked up and said, 'Father, I thank you for having heard me,' and cried, 'Lazarus, come out!' The dead man came out, his hands and feet bound with strips of cloth, and his face wrapped in a cloth. Jesus said to them, 'Unbind him, and let him go.' The chief priests and the Pharisees called a meeting of the council, and said, 'What are we to do?' Caiaphas, who was high priest that year, said, 'It is better to have one man die for the people than to have the whole nation destroyed.'

14

Jerusalem

Jesus and his followers were approaching Jerusalem. Jesus sent two disciples and said, 'Go into the village and bring a colt that has never been ridden.' They brought it to Jesus and threw their cloaks on it and he sat on it. Many people spread their cloaks on the road, and others spread leafy branches that they had cut in the fields. Then those who went ahead and those who followed were shouting, 'Hosanna! Blessed is the one who comes in the name of the Lord! Blessed is the coming kingdom of David! Hosanna in the highest heaven!' Then he entered Jerusalem and went into the temple. He drove out those who were buying and selling and overturned the tables of the money-changers and the seats of those who sold doves. He was saying, 'Is it not written, "My house shall be called a house of prayer for all the nations"? But you have made it a den of robbers.' When the chief priests and the scribes heard it, they kept looking for a way to kill him; for they were afraid of him, because the whole crowd was spellbound by his teaching.

Then he said, 'A man planted a vineyard, put a fence around it, dug a pit for the wine press, and built a watch-tower; then he leased it to tenants and went to another country. When the season came, he sent a slave to the tenants to collect from them his share of the produce of the vineyard. But they seized him, and beat him, and sent him away empty-handed. And again he sent another slave to them; this one they beat over the head. The third one they killed. And so it was with many others; some they beat, and others they killed. He had still one other, a beloved son. Finally he sent him to them, saying, "They will respect my son." But those tenants said to one another, "This is the heir; come, let us kill him, and the inheritance will be ours." So they seized him, killed him, and threw him out of the vineyard. What then will the owner of the vineyard do? He will come and destroy the tenants and give the vineyard to others.'

Then they sent to him some Pharisees and Herodians to trap him. They said, 'Is it lawful to pay taxes to the emperor, or not?' Jesus replied, 'Bring me a denarius and let me see it.' Then he said to them, 'Whose head is this, and whose title?' They answered, 'The emperor's.' Jesus said to them, 'Give to the emperor the things that are the emperor's, and to God the things that are God's.' And they were utterly amazed.

He watched the crowd putting money into the treasury. Many rich people put in large sums. A poor widow came and put in two small copper coins, which are worth a penny. Then he called his disciples and said to them, 'Truly I tell you, this poor widow has put in more than all those who are contributing to the treasury. For all of them have contributed out of their abundance; but she out of her poverty has put in all she had to live on.'

Two days before the Passover Jesus was at Bethany in the house of Simon the leper. A woman came with an alabaster jar of very costly ointment of nard, and she broke open the jar and poured the ointment on his head. But some were there who said to one another in anger, 'Why was the ointment wasted in this way? It could have been sold for more than 300 denarii, and the money given to the poor.' But Jesus said, 'Let her alone; why do you trouble her? She has performed a good service for me. For you always have the poor with you, and you can show kindness to them whenever you wish; but you will not always have me. She has done what she could; she has anointed my body beforehand for its burial. Truly I tell you, wherever the good news is proclaimed in the whole world, what she has done will be told in remembrance of her.'

When it was time for the Passover meal, Jesus was with the twelve. And when they were eating, Jesus said, 'Truly I tell you, one of you will betray me, one who is eating with me.' Jesus took a loaf of bread, and after blessing it he broke it, gave it to them, and said, 'Take, eat; this is my body.' Then he took a cup, and after giving thanks he gave it to them, and all of them drank from it. He said to them, 'This is my blood of the covenant, which is poured out for many. Truly I tell you, I will never again drink of the fruit of the vine until that day when I drink it new in the kingdom of God.'

During supper Jesus got up from the table, took off his outer robe, and tied a towel around himself. Then he poured water into a basin and began to wash the disciples' feet and to wipe them with the towel that was tied around him. Peter said, 'Lord, you will never wash my feet.' Jesus answered, 'Unless I wash you, you have no share with me.' Simon Peter said to him, 'Lord, not my feet only but also my hands and my head!' After he had washed their feet, put on his robe, and returned to the table, Jesus said to them, 'Do you know what I have done to you? You call me Teacher and Lord – and you are right, for that is what I am. So if I, your Lord and Teacher, have washed your feet, you also ought to wash one another's feet. I give you a new commandment. Just as I have loved you, you also should love one another. By this everyone will know that you are my disciples, if you have love for one another.'

Peter said to him, 'Even though all become deserters, I will not.' Jesus said to him, 'Truly I tell you, this day, this very night, before the cock crows twice, you will deny me three times.' But he said vehemently, 'Even though I must die with you, I will not deny you.'

They went to a place called Gethsemane; and he said to his disciples, 'Sit here while I pray.' He took with him Peter and James and John, and began to be distressed and agitated. And he said to them, 'I am deeply grieved, even to death; remain here, and keep awake.' And going a little further, he threw himself on the ground and prayed that, if it were possible, the hour might pass from him. He said, 'Abba, Father, for you all things are possible; remove this cup from me; yet, not what I want, but what you will.' He found the disciples sleeping and he said to Peter, 'Are you asleep? Could you not keep awake one hour? Keep awake and pray that you may not come into the time of trial; the spirit indeed is willing, but the flesh is weak. See, my betrayer is at hand.' Immediately Judas, one of the twelve, arrived; and with him there was a crowd with swords and clubs, from the chief priests, the scribes, and the elders. Judas went up to Jesus at once and said, 'Rabbi!' and kissed him. Then they laid hands on him and arrested him. All the disciples deserted him and fled.

15

Death

They took Jesus to the high priest; and all the chief priests, the elders, and the scribes were assembled. Peter had followed him at a distance, right into the courtyard; and he was sitting with the guards, warming himself at the fire. The chief priests and the whole council were looking for testimony against Jesus to put him to death; but they found none. For many gave false testimony against him, and their testimony did not agree. The high priest asked him, 'Are you the Messiah, the Son of the Blessed One?' Jesus said, 'I am.' Then the high priest tore his clothes. All of them condemned him as deserving death.

While Peter was below in the courtyard, one of the servant-girls of the high priest came by. She said, 'You also were with Jesus.' But he denied it, saying, 'I do not know what you are talking about.' Then the cock crowed. And the servant-girl, on seeing him, began again to say to the bystanders, 'This man is one of them.' But again he denied it. Then the bystanders again said to Peter, 'Certainly you are one of them.' But he swore an oath, 'I do not know this man you are talking about.' At that moment the cock crowed for the second time. And Peter broke down and wept.

Jesus was handed over to Pontius Pilate, the Roman

governor. Pilate asked, 'Are you the King of the Jews?' Jesus answered, 'My kingdom is not from this world. I came into the world to testify to the truth. Everyone who belongs to the truth listens to my voice.' Pilate asked him, 'What is truth?' Now at the festival Pilate's custom was to release a prisoner for them. A man called Barabbas was in prison for murder during the insurrection. Pilate said, 'Do you want me to release for you the King of the Jews?' But the crowd demanded Barabbas. 'Then what do you wish me to do with the King of the Jews?' They shouted back, 'Crucify him!' Pilate asked them, 'Why, what evil has he done?' But they shouted all the more, 'Crucify him!' So Pilate, wishing to satisfy the crowd, released Barabbas for them; and after flogging Jesus, he handed him over to be crucified.

The soldiers compelled Simon of Cyrene to carry Jesus's cross. Then they brought Jesus to the place called Golgotha. They crucified him, and divided his clothes among them, casting lots. The chief priests, along with the scribes, mocked him: 'He saved others; he cannot save himself.' Jesus said, 'Father, forgive them; for they do not know what they are doing.' One of the bandits crucified with him said, 'Jesus, remember me when you come into your kingdom.' Jesus replied, 'Today you will be with me in Paradise.' Standing near the cross were Jesus' mother, and his mother's sister, Mary the wife of Clopas, and Mary Magdalene. When Jesus saw his mother and the disciple whom he loved standing beside her, he said to his mother, 'Woman, here is your son.' Then he said to the disciple, 'Here is your mother.'

Darkness came over the whole land. Jesus cried out with a loud voice, 'Eloi, Eloi, lema sabachthani?' which means, 'My God, my God, why have you forsaken me?' Then Jesus gave a loud cry and breathed his last. The curtain of the temple was torn in two, from top to bottom. The centurion, who stood facing him, said, 'Truly this man was God's Son.'

16

Pentecost

Jesus had died and been raised and ascended into heaven. After Jesus' ascension the disciples were reflecting together on who Jesus was, what had happened, and what might happen next. Suddenly from heaven there came a sound like the rush of a violent wind, and it filled the entire house where they were sitting. Divided tongues, as of fire, appeared among them, and a tongue rested on each of them. All of them were filled with the Holy Spirit and began to speak in other languages, as the Spirit gave them ability. Outside the crowd gathered for the day of Pentecost were dumbfounded, because each one said to the disciples 'You are speaking in my own language!' But Peter proclaimed, 'Jesus of Nazareth, a man attested to you by God with deeds of power, wonders, and signs that God did through him among you – this man, handed over to you according to the definite plan and foreknowledge of God, you crucified and killed by the hands of those outside the law. But God raised him up, having freed him from death, because it was impossible for him to be held in its power.'

That day 3,000 people believed. They devoted themselves to the apostles' teaching and fellowship, to the breaking of bread and the prayers. Awe came upon everyone, because many wonders and signs were being done by the apostles. The believers were together and shared all things in common; they sold their possessions and goods and distributed the proceeds to those in need. Day by day, as they spent much time together in the temple, they broke bread at home and ate their food with glad and generous hearts, praising God and having the goodwill of all the people. And daily the Lord added to their number those who were being saved.

Stephen was one of those appointed to assist in the distribution of food. Some people accused him of blasphemy and he was arrested. When he spoke before the council, the council became enraged. But Stephen's face was like that of an angel. Filled with the Holy Spirit, he gazed into heaven and saw the glory of God and Jesus standing at the right hand of God. But they dragged him out of the city and began to stone him; and the witnesses laid their coats at the feet of a young man named Saul. Stephen prayed, 'Lord Jesus, receive my spirit.' Then he cried out in a loud voice, 'Lord, do not hold this sin against them.' When he had said this, he died.

Meanwhile a Pharisee named Saul was ravaging the church by entering house after house; dragging off both men and women, he committed them to prison. He was on the road to Damascus, to persecute believers there. Suddenly a light from heaven flashed around him. He fell to the ground and heard a voice saying, 'Saul, Saul, why do you persecute me?' He asked, 'Who are you, Lord?' The reply came, 'I am Jesus, whom you are persecuting. But get up and enter the city, and you will be told what you are to do.' The men who were travelling with him stood speechless because they heard the voice but saw no one. Saul got up from the ground, and though his eyes were open, he could see nothing; so they led him by the hand and brought him into Damascus. For three days he was without sight, and neither ate nor drank.

A disciple in Damascus named Ananias laid his hands on Saul and said, 'Brother Saul, the Lord Jesus, who appeared to you on your way here, has sent me so that you may regain your sight and be filled with the Holy Spirit.' And immediately scales fell from his eyes, and his sight was restored. Then he got up and was baptized, and after taking some food, he regained his strength. He began to be known as Paul.

While in Joppa Peter fell into a trance. He saw heaven opened and a large sheet being lowered to the ground by its four corners. In it were all kinds of four-footed creatures and reptiles and birds of the air. Then he heard a voice saying, 'Get up, Peter; kill and eat.' But Peter said, 'No, Lord; for I have never eaten anything that is profane or unclean.' The voice said to him again, a second time, 'What God has made clean, you must not call profane.'

So Peter said, 'Now I understand that God shows no partiality, but in every nation anyone who does what is right is acceptable. Jesus is the one ordained by God as judge of the living and the dead. All the prophets testify about him that everyone who believes in him receives forgiveness of sins through his name.' While Peter was still speaking, the Holy Spirit fell upon all who heard his words. The circumcised believers who were with Peter were astounded that the gift of the Holy Spirit had been poured out even on the Gentiles, for they heard them speaking in tongues and extolling God. Then Peter said, 'Can anyone withhold the water for baptizing these people who have received the Holy Spirit just as we have?' So he ordered them to be baptized in the name of Jesus Christ. And the circumcised believers said, 'Then God has given even to the Gentiles the repentance that leads to life.'

Paul and Barnabas met with the apostles to discuss whether

the Gentile believers should be circumcised. Peter said, 'Why are you putting God to the test by placing on the neck of the disciples a yoke that neither our ancestors nor we have been able to bear? In cleansing the Gentiles' hearts by faith he has made no distinction between them and us.' The whole assembly listened to Barnabas and Paul as they told of all the signs and wonders that God had done through them among the Gentiles.

And so began the church – centred on Jesus, a living stone - rejected by people yet chosen and precious in God's sight and, like living stones, built into a spiritual house, a holy priesthood. This church began to see itself as a chosen race, a royal priesthood, a holy nation, God's own people, proclaiming the mighty acts of God who called them out of darkness into marvellous light.

17

Paul

Paul began to write letters to the churches across the Mediterranean. He expressed his passion for the gospel: 'I want to know Christ and the power of his resurrection and the sharing of his sufferings by becoming like him in his death, if somehow I may attain the resurrection from the dead.'

Paul showed us who Christ is: 'He is the image of the invisible God, the firstborn of all creation; all things have been created through him and for him. He himself is before all things, and in him all things hold together. He is the head of the body, the church; he is the beginning, the firstborn from the dead, so that he might come to have first place in everything. For in him all the fullness of God was pleased to dwell, and through him God was pleased to reconcile to himself all things, whether on earth or in heaven, by making peace through the blood of his cross.'

Paul described the pattern of Christ's ministry: 'Though he was in the form of God, Christ did not regard equality with God as something to be exploited, but emptied himself, taking the form of a slave, being born in human likeness. And being found in human form, he humbled himself and became obedient to the point of death – even death on a cross. Therefore God also highly exalted him and gave him the name that is above every name, that at the name of Jesus every knee should bend, in heaven and on earth and under the earth, and every tongue should confess that Jesus Christ is Lord, to the glory of God the Father.'

Following Jesus, Paul suffered greatly for the gospel. He described how, 'as servants of God we have commended ourselves in every way: through great endurance, in afflictions, hardships, calamities, beatings, imprisonments, riots, labours, sleepless nights, hunger; by purity, knowledge, patience, kindness, holiness of spirit, genuine love, truthful speech, and the power of God; with the weapons of righteousness for the right hand and for the left; in honour and dishonour, in ill repute and good repute. We are treated as impostors, and yet are true; as unknown, and yet are well known; as dying, and see – we are alive; as punished, and yet not killed; as sorrowful, yet always rejoicing; as poor, yet making many rich; as having nothing, and yet possessing everything.'

Despite all these trials, he proclaimed, 'I consider that the sufferings of this present time are not worth comparing with the glory about to be revealed to us. For the creation waits with eager longing for the revealing of the children of God. The Spirit helps us in our weakness; for we do not know how to pray as we ought, but that very Spirit intercedes with sighs too deep for words. We know that all things work together for good for those who love God. If God is for us, who is against us? God did not withhold the Son: surely God will give us everything else? Who will separate us from the love of Christ? Will hardship, or distress, or persecution, or famine, or nakedness, or peril, or sword? No, in all these things we are more than conquerors through him who loved us. For I am convinced that neither death, nor life, nor angels, nor rulers, nor things present, nor things to come, nor powers, nor height, nor depth, nor anything else in all creation, will be able to separate us from the love of God in Christ Jesus our Lord.'

Paul saw that Jesus was the embodiment of peace and reconciliation with God and one another. 'God, who is rich in mercy, out of the great love with which we were loved even when we were dead through our trespasses, made us alive together with Christ and raised us up with Christ and seated us in the heavenly places, so that in the ages to come we might see the immeasurable riches of that grace in kindness towards us in Christ Jesus. For by grace you have been saved through faith, and this is not your own doing; it is the gift of God – not the result of works, so that no one may boast. For we are created in Christ Jesus for good works, which God prepared beforehand to be our way of life.' Here is our reconciliation with God.

Paul went on, 'At one time you Gentiles were without Christ, being aliens from the commonwealth of Israel, and strangers to the covenants of promise, having no hope and without God in the world. But now in Christ Jesus you who once were far off have been brought near. For he is our peace; in his flesh he has made both groups into one and has broken down the dividing wall, that is, the hostility between us. He has abolished the law with its commandments and ordinances, so that he might create in himself one new humanity in place of the two, thus making peace, and might reconcile both groups to God in one body through the cross. Through him both of us have access in one Spirit to the Father. So you are no longer strangers and aliens, but you are citizens with the saints and members of the household of God, built upon the foundation of the apostles and prophets, with Christ Jesus himself as the cornerstone. In him the whole structure is joined together and grows into a holy temple in the Lord; in whom you also are built together spiritually into a dwelling-place for God.' Here is our peace with one another.

And this gave Paul a vision of what the church could be. 'To each is given the manifestation of the Spirit for the common good. To one is given through the Spirit the utterance of wisdom, and to another the utterance of knowledge according to the same Spirit, to another faith by the same Spirit, to another gifts of healing by the one Spirit, to another the working of miracles, to another prophecy, to another the discernment of spirits, to another various kinds of tongues, to another the interpretation of tongues. For just as the body is one and has many members, and all the members of the body, though many, are one body, so it is with Christ. The eye cannot say to the hand, "I have no need of you." On the contrary, the members of the body that seem to be weaker are indispensable, and those members of the body that we think less honourable we clothe with greater honour, and our less respectable members are treated with greater respect. But God has so arranged the body, giving the greater honour to the inferior member, that there may be no dissension within the body, but the members may have the same care for one another. If one member suffers, all suffer together with it; if one member is honoured, all rejoice together with it. Now you are the body of Christ and individually members of it. And God has appointed in the church first apostles, second prophets, third teachers; then deeds of power, then gifts of healing, forms of assistance, forms of leadership, various kinds of tongues.'

Paul showed us how to work out what is right and what truly builds up the church. He said, 'The fruit of the Spirit is love, joy, peace, patience, kindness, generosity, faithfulness, gentleness, and self-control. There is no law against such things. If we live by the Spirit, let us also be guided by the Spirit.' Paul pleaded with believers, 'You were called to freedom; only do not use your freedom as an opportunity for self-indulgence, but through love become slaves to one another. For the whole law is summed up in a single commandment, "You shall love your neighbour as yourself."'

And Paul told us to love as God loves. 'Love is patient; love is kind; love is not envious or boastful or arrogant or rude. It does not insist on its own way; it is not irritable or resentful; it does not rejoice in wrongdoing, but rejoices in the truth. It bears all things, believes all things, hopes all things, endures all things. Love never ends. Now we see in a mirror, dimly, but then we will see face to face. Now I know only in part; then I will know fully, even as I have been fully known. And now faith, hope, and love abide, these three; and the greatest of these is love.'

18

Revelation

Alone on Patmos John saw that the power of Babylon and Rome had become one with the power of Satan, and that God would ultimately bring history to an end. And just as Christ had brought heaven and earth into perfect union, so at the end of time God would make a new heaven and a new earth in which to dwell with humanity forever. John in his vision saw a great multitude that no one could count, from every nation, from all tribes and peoples and languages, standing before the throne and before the Lamb, robed in white, with palm branches in their hands. They cried out in a loud voice, 'Salvation belongs to our God who is seated on the throne, and to the Lamb!' And all the angels stood around the throne and around the elders and the four living creatures, and they fell on their faces before the throne and worshipped God, singing, 'Blessing and glory and wisdom and thanksgiving and honour and power and might be to our God for ever and ever!'

Then John saw, robed in white, those who had come out of the great ordeal; they had washed their robes and made them white in the blood of the Lamb. They were before the throne of God, worshipping him day and night within the temple. They would hunger no more, and thirst no more; the sun would not strike them, nor any scorching heat; for the Lamb at the centre of the throne was their shepherd, to guide them to springs of the water of life, and God would wipe away every tear from their eyes.

Finally John saw a new heaven and a new earth; for the first heaven and the first earth had passed away, and the sea was no more. And he saw the holy city, the new Jerusalem, coming down out of heaven from God, prepared as a bride adorned for her husband. And he heard a loud voice from the throne saying, 'See, the home of God is among mortals. God will dwell with them and be with them; he will wipe every tear from their eyes. Death will be no more; mourning and crying and pain will be no more. The first things have passed away.' And the one who was seated on the throne said, 'I am making all things new. I am the Alpha and the Omega, the beginning and the end. To the thirsty I will give water as a gift from the spring of the water of life.' Jerusalem had the glory of God and a radiance like a very rare jewel, like jasper, clear as crystal. John saw no temple in the city, for its temple is the Lord God the Almighty and the Lamb. The city has no need of sun or moon to shine on it, for the glory of God is its light, and its lamp is the Lamb. The nations will walk by its light, and the kings of the earth will bring their glory into it. Its gates will never be shut by day – and there will be no night there. People will bring into it the glory and the honour of the nations.

Then an angel showed John the river of the water of life, bright as crystal, flowing from the throne of God and of the Lamb through the middle of the street of the city. On either side of the river is the tree of life with its 12 kinds of fruit, producing its fruit each month. The leaves of the tree are for the healing of the nations. Nothing accursed will be found there anymore. But the throne of God and of the Lamb will be in it, and his servants will worship him; they will see his face, and his name will be on their foreheads. And there will be no more night; they need no light of lamp or sun, for the Lord God will be their light, and they will reign for ever and ever.

Commentary

Introduction

The people who wrote the Bible didn't know they were writing the Bible. The church has always believed that the Holy Spirit guided the hand of the writers; but of those who were writing, very few were self-consciously aware that they were composing what today we regard as 'the Scriptures'. They were ensuring that the treasured experience of their people was recorded for wider dissemination and for future generations. In almost every case, it was the hand of later compilers and editors that recognized a sacred thread of story and tradition of which the original writers were only partly aware.

I believe it's appropriate to set out the diverse literature of the 66 books of the Bible as a story, and a story that crosses both Testaments, even though much of the material is not set out in narrative form. For example, the Psalms appear as simply a book of songs, while Paul's writings are set out as a series of letters, with no assistance given to order them by theme or date of writing. Proverbs is largely a collection of epigrams. Leviticus is mostly made up of laws. Ecclesiastes is a series of mellow reflections. But such non-narrative elements in almost every case presuppose a story, which Christians see broadly as follows:

God created the world, called a people, delivered that people from slavery, made a covenant with them, gave them land, king and temple, watched them stray and go into exile, and brought them home. God then came among them in Jesus, and Jesus portrayed the kingdom of God through word and action; but he was put to death, only for God to raise him, and take him to heaven, after which God sent the Holy Spirit to empower a church that opened God's life out to all the peoples of the earth, which it continues to do as it anticipates the last day, on which God will unveil and install the everlasting kingdom.

But I don't set out the story in this form in the foregoing account. It's not a seamless account. It's a story that, in each of its two parts, starts in the middle. In both Old and New Testaments there's a decisive event that accounts for the recording of the story, and in both cases I decided that the story should start with that decisive event, and thus begin in the middle, only subsequently to incorporate the 'beginning' of the story, which in each case only makes sense in the light of the decisive event.

In the Old Testament the decisive event is Israel's exile in Babylon. This is the catastrophe that turns out to be the refiner's fire. Babylon becomes the crucible of Israel's story, because in the light of the loss of land, king and temple, the exiles come to realize they need to write down their story in order to assess what they haven't lost. And it becomes the crucible also of Israel's future, because the answer they find is that what they haven't lost is God – indeed they begin to recognize that they've discovered a new, more intimate, more personal face of God. The God whom the early church worshipped as being present in Jesus is almost unimaginable without the transformation that took place in the Exile five centuries earlier. And so I begin the book with the story of the fiery furnace, because that story epitomizes the Exile, and the new notion of a God who is fundamentally *with* Israel, rather than a God who is assumed to be always *for* Israel. The God who is for Israel is primarily a benefactor; the God who is with Israel is primarily a companion.

In the New Testament the decisive event is the resurrection of Jesus Christ. It's impossible to imagine the Old Testament being written without the Exile; it's impossible to imagine the New Testament being written without Jesus' resurrection. I begin Part Two with Paul in exile, to underline the correspondence with Part One; but the first section is really about the resurrection, the astonishing event that transformed a group of weary, frightened disciples into a dynamic team of empowered apostles, clothed by the Spirit and set to go into all the world. In a subtler way I seek to bring out the manner in which the New Testament consciously echoes the Old: Jesus is brought to Egypt by Joseph, just as Israel is; he begins his ministry at the Jordan, just as Israel entered the Promised Land there; he spends 40 days in the wilderness, as Israel had spent 40 years; he calls 12 disciples, as Israel had 12 tribes; he hands down a new law on a mountain, as Moses had received the old law on a mountain; he becomes the lamb of God, just as the Passover lamb had epitomized Israel's deliverance; and so on.

Part One

Part One begins with fire, because I want to recognize that Babylon was a crucible in which a refiner's fire left Israel with a much clearer idea of who it was and who God was. But the first section is really about water, because Israel came into being most explicitly in the crossing of the Red Sea to escape Egypt and the crossing of the Jordan to enter the Promised Land. And Christians recall these two events as the fundamental constituents of baptism, which itself marks the beginning of Christian identity. The burning bush links the theme of fire to that of water by initiating the chain of events that led Moses to the seabed of the Red Sea and to the verge of Jordan. Between the Red Sea and the Jordan lies the wilderness. Just as Israel was refined by the 50 years of Exile, it was defined by those 40 years in the wilderness. The wilderness was about one question: was Israel prepared to depend utterly on God? That's the question that runs through the whole of the Old Testament.

Covenant is perhaps the single most important word in the whole of the Old Testament, and so it becomes the theme of the second section of the narrative. Covenant is about the permanent intersection of the holiness of God with the fitful faithfulness and wanton waywardness of Israel. I regard the covenant with Moses as the definitive covenant, in the light of which other covenants – Noah, Abraham, David – take their place. The covenant section includes stories from Joshua and Judges of how Israel took and kept possession of the Promised Land, to demonstrate the covenant in action: the more Israel depends on God alone, the more remarkable are the events that ensue. Part of the balance is that God's covenant is never narrowly for Israel's own sake. It's always for the sake of the world. Covenant is always a gift and a commission and never a possession or an entitlement. The purpose is always the restoration of creation and its companionship with God: Noah was one way of doing this, Abraham another, and Moses and David elaborated on what was undertaken with Abraham. Jesus is in continuity with this tradition of covenant – still for the sake of God being with creation.

I consistently use the word 'we' for two reasons: first, because Israel sees itself in a kind of perpetual present tense in its covenant with God – all parts of the story are always in an animated memory, not a forgotten past; and second, because Christians need to read the Bible recalling that the Jews were the original 'we', and if Christians adopt that 'we', they need to do so in a way that never makes the Jews a 'they'. Christians are grafted into a story that was originally about Israel and never ceases to be. That's what I mean to convey by using the pronoun 'we'.

The third section tells of how the notion of covenant expanded in the person of the king and the building of the temple. A king was partly a pragmatic step (Judges repeatedly laments that the result of having no ruler was chaos and national vulnerability) but also a desire to embody the promises and faithfulness of God in one individual, as became fully realized in Jesus. I have tried to represent how 'covenant' came to mean several different things; just as 'story' covers many kinds of Old Testament literature, so covenant covers several nuances of how Israel related to God and understood its destiny. The details of how Solomon constructed the temple are important because they are all ways of expressing that Israel's prosperity had a purpose – building God's house.

This is, then, the context in which to describe Israel's fall from grace. The story of Adam and Eve comes at the beginning of Genesis, the first book of the Bible. But I chose to place it here, in order to highlight its role in relation to how the Bible came to be written. The story of David and Bathsheba is as emblematic for the fall of Israel as the story of Eve, the serpent and Adam is for the fall of humankind. David, like Israel, has the world at his feet; but he wants the one thing he can't have, just as Eve and Adam do. Again, the key is to perceive how this story looks from the perspective of the exiles in Babylon 400 years later, coming to terms with how Israel lost its glory and almost lost everything. There are many stories that could illustrate how things went astray from the waywardness of David onwards, not least in the split between the northern and southern kingdoms and the apostasy of some of the kings thereafter. But I regard the account of the death of Absalom and David's grief as the most moving passage in the Bible, and it takes an appropriate place here.

The distressing infidelity of many generations of kings and peoples is the natural place to describe the ministry of the prophets. Israel had no notion of the separation of church and state; thus the prophets blended what we might think of as a religious role with a social/political one. Their message was simple: it called Israel and Judah back to explicit dependence on God, and as a test of that faithfulness it observed the way contemporary society treated the widow, the orphan and the stranger. A great deal of the Old Testament is prophecy – indeed the traditional division is between the Law, the Prophets, and the Writings, which makes it clear that what are often thought of as history books – 1 and 2 Samuel, 1 and 2 Kings, for example –

are simply different forms of prophecy. Prophecy doesn't mean prediction – it means holding up the woes of the present in the light of God's words and actions in the past and demanding a future more in line with God's character, here disclosed in the covenant.

The Old Testament portrays the Exile as the result of Israel's sin, so the logical way to present the narrative is for Exile to follow prophecy, brought about by Israel's collective failure to mend its ways even under the prophetic counsel of a host of figures such as Elijah, Hosea, Amos and Micah. The Bible has no lengthy, detailed account of the destruction of Jerusalem, still less of the march to Babylon, and almost nothing concerning those left behind in Jerusalem. But the principal facts about the end of the kingdom need telling, and are rendered in the Old Testament in various forms, notably Lamentations. This is the definitive moment of lament in the Bible. Lament is where the reality of a situation is brought into direct contrast with the covenant grace of God, and the speaker looks to God to reduce the glaring gap between the two. Presenting the Exile here, having anticipated it at the outset of the story, is a way of returning to the place we first started and knowing it for the first time.

Part One finishes with the return. It's a complex, unfulfilled, untidy picture. Some never returned – the story of Esther is the most vivid portrayal of this dynamic; and Esther provides the most explicit foreshadowing of Christ in the whole of the Old Testament. Many did return, under Ezra and Nehemiah: it wasn't a single event, like the Exodus or the Exile, but a process that stretched over many decades. And what the returnees found wasn't the same as what they'd left. They did rebuild the walls, they did build a new temple; they did dream of a future bigger than the past. But the ark of the covenant was gone, the sense of being fully reconciled with God was incomplete, the presence of occupying powers was all around them. It was a half-return.

I complete Part One with Psalm 23 because that most familiar of psalms is invariably read as a personal statement of faith in the face of sunshine and rain; but in the light of the story just told, it emerges as an overarching narrative that embraces the green pastures of faithful times and the valley of the shadow of fear and despair – indeed, as a vision of the whole of the Old Testament in one song.

Part Two

Like Part One, Part Two begins in exile. It could perhaps have begun with John on Patmos, writing the book of Revelation. But Revelation is such a mysterious book and its style is out of step with the style and ethos of most of the New Testament, so I chose instead to begin with Paul, whose journey to ultimate death in Rome in many respects echoes and imitates Jesus' journey to death in Jerusalem. Exile is the characteristic outlook of the Bible, because people of faith are very much aware of what God has done and of the wonders of God's grace, but they often find their circumstances cry out for God to act again and they long for God to be present with them in the midst of their struggles. It is not that God seems to have moved far away from them, it's that, through either misfortune or mischief, they seem to be far removed from God.

But the beginning of Part Two is designed to set up a contrast that reflects the reality of the early church, within which the New Testament was written. The early church faced persecution, hardship, setback; and yet it rejoiced in the glory of Christ's resurrection. So quickly I set down precisely some of the recollections of the first Easter morning, because these are the cherished words on which for Christians the whole of biblical faith rests: he is risen. The resurrection is described in various ways in the New Testament, across several books, and the different accounts are hard to reconcile in a continuous narrative, either sequentially or geographically. But what is without question is that for Christians they collectively constitute the most precious words ever recorded, and so it is appropriate to begin with them. One contemporary theologian describes faith thus: 'God is whoever raised Jesus from the dead, having before raised Israel from Egypt' (Robert Jenson, *Systematic Theology*, Volume 1, p. 63). The ascension of Christ is an even more mysterious event, but in Matthew's account it is associated with Jesus' words inaugurating the mission of the church, and so it makes a fitting climax to the first section of Part Two.

The place to begin the story thereafter is with the annunciation. Once upon a time the calendar year began on 25 March, nine months before Christmas Day – because the coming of Jesus is a new creation. Indeed Matthew's account begins with the Greek word 'genesis' – a clear indication of this understanding. Incarnation plays the same role in the New Testament that covenant plays in the Old: it's the embodiment of God's faithfulness and the guarantee that there is no destiny for God separable from the commitment to be with Israel and the creation. The different scriptural accounts place this central event in the context of Old Testament hopes, ancient lineage back to David, Abraham and

Adam, Israel's subjection to Roman rule, and the intimate relations of the Trinity before the beginning of time.

Jesus' baptism and temptations set the tone for the whole of his ministry. The baptism is perhaps the clearest signal of all that Jesus is taking on the mantle of Israel: beginning his ministry at the Jordan is a way of rebooting Israel's story, and since the name Jesus is the equivalent of the name Joshua, he starts where Joshua started. In his temptations Jesus inhabits the threefold expectations of being prophet (performing miracles), priest (at the temple) and king (ruling the nations) – thus again reinventing what it means to embody Israel's story. I have chosen to focus on the Sermon on the Mount, Matthew 5–7, since summarizing Jesus' teaching is such a challenge. Here Jesus, like a new Moses, makes a new covenant by redefining what the law really entails. The Beatitudes have been described as the most important words spoken by the most important person who ever lived: they deserve a prominent place.

Much of Jesus' teaching is in parables, and I have given a whole section to parables because they convey so much of the flavour of the first three gospels. The mistake in reading the parables is to treat Jesus as Aesop and look too quickly for a moral. The secret is to perceive how in most cases the parable is talking about God, and more specifically about Jesus himself. Thus in the parable of the last judgement the key is to recognize that when Jesus talks about the hungry, thirsty, naked, stranger, sick, and prisoner, he himself has been or will be each of these things. In the parable of the Good Samaritan, Jesus is the one who comes to us in our plight and restores us, heals us, gives us safe lodging and promises to return. In the parable of the labourers in the vineyard, Jesus is the one who pays us the wages of forgiveness and eternal life, such that it's absurd for anyone to feel entitled to more forgiveness or more eternal life than their neighbour. In the parable of the prodigal son, Jesus is the one who makes the journey out to welcome the younger brother and the journey into the field to invite the elder brother. In the parable of the merchant, Jesus is the one who sells everything and we are the pearl for which he does so. The parables are not primarily ethics, telling us how to live: they are theology, showing us who God is.

The miracles are like enacted parables. When Jesus heals the paralytic, it's like he's depicting how he's delivering Israel from its paralysis and putting it back on its feet again. When he feeds the 5,000, he's offering a model of how God turns our scarcity (the loaves and fish) into abundance (the 12 baskets left over) and empowers the church (the disciples) to make the whole world a Eucharist of thanksgiving and sharing (the result of Jesus' fourfold action of taking, blessing, breaking and giving). When he heals the Gerasene demoniac, he contrasts how the many (pigs) die for the one (Legion), whereas shortly the one (he himself) will die for the many. When he raises Lazarus from the dead, he foreshadows how he himself will go into the place of horror and impurity because out of great love he longs to bring us out of the tomb of death.

The account of Jesus' passion in Jerusalem weaves together the intimacy of the Last Supper, Judas' betrayal, and Peter's denial, with the wider canvas of Roman occupation, the authorities' duplicity, and the great movements of the heavens and the earth. Mark's gospel has been called a passion narrative with a long introduction, and there's no question that the gospels see the last week in Jerusalem as the focus of Jesus' whole ministry.

It's the time par excellence when we see the wonder of who God is and the truth of who we are. The three strands of Jesus' story – the close relationship with the twelve, the wider engagement with the crowds, and the constant disputes with the authorities – coalesce in the events of these days.

The description of Jesus' crucifixion does not concentrate on the gruesome physical details. The true horror lies in the cry of dereliction. Jesus has been abandoned by those who should have celebrated his coming – the authorities – by the fickle crowds, and by those who knew him and loved him best, the disciples. Now he is, it seems, abandoned also by his Father. This is a scene of utter desolation, opening the chasm of fear that Jesus' birth and ministry has been in vain. It seems to be with us Jesus must face being without the Father; and to allow Jesus to be with us the Father must be without Jesus. It is the most intimate and yet cosmic moment imaginable – and the most vivid portrayal of what it means for God to keep the covenant in the face of our infidelity. Among many ironies, Jesus, son of the Father, is rejected in favour of Barabbas, whose name means son of the father; while Rome, in the person of the centurion, realizes who Jesus really is, but only at the point of his death.

Like Part One, Part Two is written in such a way that the context in which the story begins, in this case the resurrection, re-enters the narrative around four-fifths of the way through, making sense for the first time. Resurrection isn't the end of the story, however: the body of Christ on earth is to be the church, which is founded and empowered by the dramatic events of Pentecost. The Holy Spirit makes Christ present and clothes the church with grace to live the redeemed life and power to share the gospel with the nations. A crucial development that is described in the Acts of the Apostles is how Jesus' mission to renew Israel and make it ready to come face to face with God becomes a gospel to be taken to the Gentiles and to bring the whole creation around the throne of grace. Gone was any sense that the community was restricted by nation, tongue or race: this was the overflowing love of God for all creation, embodied in a community that sought to reflect back that love in every aspect of its life.

It's not the purpose of a narrative treatment to attempt to systematize Paul's thought. More important is to get a sense of how the letters fit with the story told in the Acts of the Apostles – of how in word and deed Paul was energetically bringing the faith to different parts of the Mediterranean and tirelessly encouraging and guiding the young churches as they faced abiding questions and local controversies. Paul shows us the heart of what God was doing in Christ; but he also describes the workings of the Holy Spirit as it forms and renews the church. Like Jesus he faces the consequences of living wholly for God in an environment that is sometimes allergic to God's ways: but such adversity only refines the truth that he longs to share.

The question about Revelation is, as with all reflection and anticipation of the end times, whether precise attention to how God will vindicate the oppressed and judge the living and the dead risks drawing the focus away from what God has already done in Christ. One can read Revelation as an elaborate series of stages that precede the breaking-in of God's kingdom, or as a sign of how much of a struggle the church must be prepared to face before God finally brings the story to an end. In this short treatment I have taken the latter course, seeing the coming of the New Jerusalem as the outworking of the logic of Christ's resurrection. The resurrection reprises creation and rehearses the last day; thus Part Two begins with the resurrection of Christ and ends with the resurrection of all things in God's good time.

Epilogue: The Magnificent Seven

John 21.11–18

Each year on New Year's Eve I gather round the dinner table with family and friends and we give each other time and space to remember and describe the best day of the year just gone. It's not always the happiest or the most memorable, but often the day that just had everything – the day that summed up the previous 12 months.

I want today to ask you to imagine that you've joined the communion of saints and as a bit of after-banquet fun in heaven you're going to look back on eternity and select the very best day of them all. In the manner of Britain's Got Talent or Love Island or Bake Off I'm going to suggest six finalists and consider their merits. Let's take them in chronological order.

How about the day of creation? It's got fabulous fireworks. It's got exponential imagination. It's got planets, stars, sun, moon, skies and seas, and it's got microbes, insects and electrons. There's literally nothing in the whole universe it hasn't got. It's the day the inner imagination of God got externalized and turned into tangible form. Do you think the whole history of the universe was contained in embryo on this day, like a tiny egg that contains a person's whole future?

Our second candidate is the day of the Exodus. This is the day the Old Testament looks back on as the great day when God recreated Israel, when Israel found freedom from slavery and was awestruck by the power and purpose of God. In terms of a party, it would be hard to beat the joy when Israel landed on the eastern shore of the Red Sea, and Miriam led the dancing. Just imagine the collective joy and discovery that nothing was impossible with God. Great day.

Our third candidate was the central moment in the Old Testament, the moment that everything prior had built up to and everything after had looked back to. This is the day of the covenant, when God gave Moses the law and God's commitment to Israel was crystallized in promises and guarantees and tangible forms of loyalty and love. It was the day that defined what it meant to be God's people and how to live forever in peace with God and one another. It was the original mountain-top experience.

Then to our fourth candidate. You could call it Christmas if you like – or if you're a Catholic you'd maybe go back nine months and call it the Annunciation of Gabriel to Mary. Either way, it's the day of incarnation. The day we discovered that God loved us so much as to become one like us. The day we discovered that God affirmed creation so deeply that, despite our sin, God thought it was worth entering our life, taking on our mantle, and inhabiting our existence. The day that every single day since creation had been building up to, because the Incarnation was the reason for creation. God made the world in order to be with us in Christ.

But there's another candidate lurking in the shadows. Good Friday. On the day of the Exodus Israel saw God's power. On

Good Friday we see God's love. Hands that threw stars into space to cruel nails surrendered.

The little girl used to bring home friends from school. They would play in the living room. But her father began to notice that she stopped bringing friends home to play. So he sat down on the stairs with her. He said, 'I've noticed you don't bring friends home to play anymore. Is it because of your mum?' The girl nodded. 'Is it because of her hands?' She nodded again. 'Let me tell you how your mum got those hands. One day when you were a very little girl she was next door and heard you screaming. You'd crawled into the fire. So she plunged her hands into the fire to get you out. But her hands were badly damaged. So when you see your mum's hands, you see how much she loves you.' A week or two later the father noticed his daughter started bringing friends home again. And one day he overheard her say to a friend, 'You see my mum's hands? They show how much she loves me.' That's Good Friday. What wondrous love. Could any day surpass this?

Well, here's a candidate. What about the last day. The last day of all. The day when Christ comes back. The day when everything that's been wrong in all the history of time gets set right, when all who've been downtrodden are sat on thrones, and all who've lost their lives in tragedy find untold joy. The day when evil is finally expunged and sin can plague us no more. The day when everything that creation was meant to be but never quite became is transformed and creation is restored, iridescent, changed from glory into glory and showered in wonder, love and praise. Beat that.

Well, I think we can beat that. I've laid out for you six grand finalists, all of which, in their different ways, had an audience.

Creation had the panoply of the firmament. Exodus had the applauding Israelites and terrified Egyptians. Covenant had Moses on the mountain and the children of Israel below. Christmas has oxen, asses, sheep, shepherds and kings, plus the whole heavenly host. Good Friday had mockers, passers-by, and a few crestfallen disciples. The Last Day has as its astonished spectators the whole of creation from Genesis to the maps. But the day I'm going to tell you about had almost no one to witness it.

Early in the morning, depending on which gospel you read, there was one woman, or three, or two men, who went to a tomb. It's a day that began as one of the saddest-ever days. But before breakfast time it had turned into the Day of Days – not just the greatest day of them all, but the day that contained all the other six. Just see how this day, this holiest, most astonishing and wondrous day, is all the other six days wrapped into one.

It's another creation day, because look, it's Jesus and Mary, a man and a woman in a garden, just like creation, and it's a day of limitless possibility. It's almost literally the first day – the first day of Christianity, of the past released by forgiveness and the future unleashed by eternal life. It's the beginning of everything. It's the Great Day.

And look, it's another exodus. The Israelites were led out of the slavery of the Egyptians: we, this day, are set free from evil, sin and death. It's the Exodus again but not just for a small number of people long ago but this time now, for everyone, forever. It's the end of the night of suffering and misery and the dawn of the eternal day of glory, hope and joy.

And see how it's another covenant. The first covenant came with smoke and earthquake and fire. This one too came with portents surrounding Christ's death and an earthquake that moved the stone. The first covenant showed Israel how to stay close to God: this one shows everyone that nothing can separate us from the love of God – not even death itself. Whatever we throw at God, however deeply we reject God, however much we seek to bury or destroy God, God will find a way back to us. That's the truest covenant of all.

And look how it's like the Incarnation all over again, but bigger. Christmas affirms the fleshly, tangible earthiness of human existence. Easter does so again, but this time after humanity has demonstrated one almighty allergic reaction to the goodness of God. Everything the Incarnation proclaims and embodies, the resurrection affirms twice over: God will be with us in Christ, not just out of primordial purpose, but even when we have done our absolute darnedest to expunge Christ from our presence. Resurrected life is bodily. The human body has an eternal destiny.

And most obviously, Easter is Good Friday again. Jesus shows his disciples his hands and his side. He is the good shepherd who has laid down his life for his sheep. And now this blessed morning he begins to go around reassembling his flock, starting with Mary Magdalene. Good Friday shows us that God will be with us even if it splits God's heart in two, even if it threatens to sever the inner-Trinitarian relationship of the Father and the Son. Easter shows us that nothing whatsoever can stop God being with us, not just at the most intense moment in history – but forever.

And then finally Easter is everything the Last Day will be, but in microcosm. Like the Last Day, Easter restores creation. Like the Last Day, Easter vindicates the oppressed, in this case

Jesus, and exalts the humble and meek. Like the Last Day, Easter is the enactment of every single one of the Beatitudes. Jesus is the pure in heart. Jesus is the peacemaker. Jesus is the one who hungers and thirsts for righteousness. Jesus is the one who is reviled by all people. And on the day of resurrection he's happy, he's blessed, he's called God's child, he's laughing.

This day, this wondrous, glorious, blessed, fabulous day – this day is the greatest day in the history of the universe and the story of heaven. This is the perfect seventh day, the day that comprises and epitomizes and embodies and expresses all the other six great days of all time. This is the day in which all the suffering, all the imagination, all the love, all the freedom, all the grief, all the justice, all the hope, all the wonder are combined in a mixing bowl, left behind a huge stone, and like yeast acting on a mixture, burst out, push that stone away because there's so much life there nothing can keep it in, no one can keep it down, no force in heaven or earth can stop it now.

This is the day. This is the great day. This is the glorious day. This is creation, liberation, incarnation, and consummation all wrapped into one. This is the day when we stand on the shoulders of God, and say, 'I can see forever!' This is Easter Day.

Study Guide

Week One: Part One, Chapters 1–4

Read the four chapters.

Read also the following scripture passages:

- Daniel 3
- Isaiah 43.1–7
- Exodus 3.1–15
- Genesis 32.22–31
- 1 Samuel 8.1–18
- Genesis 3.1–13

Ponder these wonderings together (remember wonderings are not questions that have right and wrong answers, but invitations to explore deeper):

- I wonder if you have ever been in exile.
- I wonder how Israel kept its faith after it had lost land, king and temple.
- I wonder if the worst thing that could happen can ever turn out to be the beginning of something new.
- I wonder what it's like to hear God say, 'I am enough for you.'
- I wonder whether Israel wanting a king was a sign of faith or unfaith.

- I wonder what it was like to carry the ark of the covenant into the temple.
- I wonder whether God knew there would be a Fall.

A closing prayer

Faithful God, you led your people out of slavery and revealed yourself as their creator; walk with any who are in the midst of fire and water and storm today.

Inscribe on our hearts the ways you are enough for us.

Forgive us the occasions we wrestle with your angel, and with our own. And give us the joy of being your children, precious, honoured and loved.

In Christ your son our Lord. Amen.

Week Two: Part One, Chapters 5–8

Read the four chapters.

Read also the following scripture passages:

- 1 Kings 19.1–16
- Hosea 6.1–6
- Jeremiah 31.31–34
- Psalm 139.1–18
- Lamentations 3.1–23
- Nehemiah 8

Ponder these wonderings together:

- I wonder what it's like to love and love and love and get little, if anything, back.
- I wonder to what extent care for the destitute is a test of true religion.
- I wonder who the baals (false gods) are today.

- I wonder if you have had a goodbye as painful as Elijah and Elisha.
- I wonder how you have coped when everything has gone calamitously wrong.
- I wonder whether someone you didn't know ended up being the agent of your salvation.
- I wonder whether God has been more present to you in green pasture, refreshing waters, or places of danger.

A closing prayer

God of truth and justice, in your prophets you showed us your will and in exile you showed your people your true heart. Visit your children when they feel all is lost; bring renewal to your people when they are learning to dream again. And make your church a community of faith, hope, and love.

In Christ your son our Lord. Amen.

Week Three: Part Two, Chapters 9–11

Read the three chapters.

Read also the following scripture passages:

- Matthew 28
- Luke 24
- John 20.1—21.19
- Acts 1.1–11
- Matthew 5—7

Ponder these wonderings together:

- I wonder what the resurrection of Jesus Christ means to you.

- I wonder what it meant for Jesus to say 'I am with you always' when he was about to leave.
- I wonder what the virgin birth really means.
- I wonder what it's like to hear God say, 'You are my beloved child.'
- I wonder what it means to 'fish for people'.
- I wonder what it means for the kingdom of heaven to come near.
- I wonder how it's possible not to judge.

A closing prayer

God of new life, you came among us in your son Jesus
and you gave us hope in his resurrection from the dead.
Open our hearts to the joy of your glory, that when we like Paul
are in chains, we may still rejoice in the promise of life with you.
Through Jesus Christ our Lord. Amen.

Week Four: Part Two, Chapters 12–15

Read the four chapters.
Read also the following scripture passages:

- Matthew 20.1–16
- John 4.5–42
- John 9
- Mark 14.1–9
- John 13.1–15
- Matthew 27.11–56

Ponder these wonderings together:

- I wonder who the parables are really about.

- I wonder who the merchant is, and who the pearl is.
- I wonder whether Jesus ever felt lonely.
- I wonder whether you would step out of the boat and walk across the water to Jesus.
- I wonder which was harder for Jesus, the physical pain or the personal betrayal.
- I wonder whether Jesus was forsaken by his Father.

A closing prayer

God of love, in Jesus you show us who you are and who we are.
Give us grateful hearts for the wondrous love he shows us
in laying down his life for those he loved.
Lead us to repent of the sins that took Jesus to the cross.
And make us part of the new family of your coming kingdom.
In Christ we pray. Amen.

Week Five: Part Two, Chapters 16–18

Read the three chapters.

Read also the following scripture passages:

- Acts 15.1–21
- Romans 3.21–26
- Romans 5.1–21
- 1 Corinthians 1.18–25
- 1 Corinthians 11.17–34
- 2 Corinthians 4.1–15
- Ephesians 2.11–22
- Colossians 1.15–23
- Hebrews 12.18–29

Ponder these wonderings together:

- I wonder whether you would like to 'have all things in common'.
- I wonder how hard it was for Jewish disciples to realize Gentiles could be Christians.
- I wonder what it was about the gospel that made the early followers of Jesus so willing to suffer so greatly.
- I wonder what part of the body of Christ you are.
- I wonder if heaven comes to earth, or we go to heaven.
- I wonder whether you feel more drawn to the gospels or to the epistles.

A closing prayer
God of faith, hope and love,
you empower your church with the gifts of your Holy Spirit.
Inspire your children to follow in the footsteps of Paul,
in sacrificial ministry and in mission to your whole world.
Fill our imaginations with the wonder of your coming glory,
that we may be your son's body, now and forever. Amen.

Week Six: Commentary
Read the four Commentary and the Epilogue.
Read also the following scripture passages:

- Deuteronomy 26.1–11
- Psalm 126
- Nehemiah 9.6–37
- Matthew 21.33–46
- Acts 7.1–53

Ponder these wonderings together:

- I wonder what part of the story has been left out.
- I wonder who would be left out even if we had read every word of the Bible.
- I wonder whether and in what ways we read the Bible backwards.
- I wonder if there is a difference between reading the Bible and letting the Bible read you.
- I wonder whether Jesus would have come even if there had not been a Fall.
- I wonder what part of the story is about you.

A closing prayer

God of glory, you have shown us your heart and your face in the story of the Bible. By the power of your Holy Spirit, draw all people into the wonder of this story, that we may each find it a refuge in trouble, a sanctuary in bewilderment, and a joy in times of plenty. As we make your story our story, bring to fruit in us the gifts of your Spirit, that we may read, think and live with wisdom and understanding, counsel and inward strength, knowledge and true fear of you.

In Christ our Lord. Amen.